DO YOU SOMETIMES FEEL YOU ARE . . .

- ☐ Caught in a rut?
- ☐ Constantly under stress?
- ☐ Unable to maintain a positive attitude?
- ☐ Neglecting personal relationships?
- ☐ Threatened by changing times and new technologies?
- ☐ Disappointed because you haven't fulfilled your dreams?

FACE THE FUTURE:
Get What You Want From Your Career,
Your Relationships, and Your Life

THE SUCCESS BREAKTHROUGH

Other Avon Books by
Samuel A. Cypert

BELIEVE AND ACHIEVE:
W. CLEMENT STONE'S 17 PRINCIPLES OF SUCCESS

THE SUCCESS BREAKTHROUGH

GET WHAT YOU WANT FROM YOUR CAREER, YOUR RELATIONSHIPS, AND YOUR LIFE

SAMUEL A. CYPERT

AVON BOOKS ◆ NEW YORK

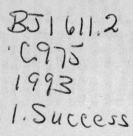
THE SUCCESS BREAKTHROUGH: GET WHAT YOU WANT FROM
YOUR CAREER, YOUR RELATIONSHIPS, AND YOUR LIFE is an
original publication of Avon Books. This work has never before appeared
in book form.

AVON BOOKS
A division of
The Hearst Corporation
1350 Avenue of the Americas
New York, New York 10019

Copyright © 1993 by Samuel A. Cypert
Published by arrangement with the author
Library of Congress Catalog Card Number: 93–90325
ISBN: 0–380–77151–9

First Avon Books Printing: October 1993

AVON TRADEMARK REG. U.S. PAT. OFF. AND IN OTHER COUNTRIES, MARCA
REGISTRADA, HECHO EN U.S.A.

Printed in the U.S.A.

RA   10   9   8   7   6   5   4   3   2   1

To my mother,
who taught me to dream impossible dreams,
and to the memory of Robert Anderson,
who taught me how to turn dreams into reality.

Contents

3   What Is a Family?   35

4   A Firm Foundation   49

5   Evolution: From Carnegie to Today   63

15   Trust, Empowerment, and Delegation   197

16   Your Anchor   212

17   A Creative Life   226

Preface

It has been my good fortune over the years to work with an exceptional group of people. Because of my interest in writing about success and successful individuals, I have had the opportunity to interview—and in many cases get to know—men and women whose names have become household words.

One who had an immeasurable influence upon my work and who has contributed greatly to the success of others is W. Clement Stone. The founder of Combined Insurance (since merged to become Aon Corporation), he has spent the past several decades spreading the philosophy of success through positive thinking. His own life is a living testimonial to the validity of his beliefs. With little more than $100 and a Positive Mental Attitude, he built his company from nothing into a giant multinational corporation.

I met Mr. Stone through Robert Anderson, former editor of *Success!*, a magazine Mr. Stone cofounded with Napoleon Hill to provide regular infusions of positive thinking to those interested in improving themselves. When Mr. Stone and I collaborated on *Believe and Achieve*, Bob Anderson was the book's editor. Bob died suddenly a few years ago, but his influence continues to be felt by the many writers he developed. His encouragement helped many of us to persevere when the going was tough.

Another whose quiet support has been invaluable is Mike Ritt, executive director of The Napoleon Hill Foundation. Mike prefers to allow others to stand in the spotlight, but he helped launch Og Mandino, Dennis Kimbro, and this writer, among others.

It was during the research for *Believe and Achieve* and other writing projects for The Napoleon Hill Foundation that I began to develop the thesis that led to this book. In conversations with Mr. Stone and other achievers it became increasingly apparent to me that the true riches of life cannot be measured in monetary terms alone.

Money is an essential ingredient of success to be sure, but when a certain comfort level is reached, it loses its allure. After he acquired all the money he needed, Mr. Stone developed a new mission in life: to make this a better world for this and future generations. He has given millions to worthy causes around the world.

Others have followed similar patterns or found new ways to motivate themselves. Some take great joy in developing young people, in helping them to grow into tomorrow's achievers. Still others, like former Gannett chief Allen Neuharth, retire to a tree house to write books.

My association with such achievers has convinced me that total success requires striking a correct balance between careers, families, relationships, and other important aspects of our lives. When we become obsessed with a single segment of our lives, we place other aspects of it in peril.

This book is about that balance.

Introduction

Someone once observed that there is really nothing new under the sun. Everything that appears new is nothing more than a modification of one of very few original ideas. I prefer to believe that everything is new—or at least in a constant state of change. It's just that the changes may occur so gradually that we do not notice them until some event or idea comes along to shake us out of our complacency.

It is also true that the more things change, the more they remain the same. All life in our cosmos seems to operate in cycles and we human beings react to cycles, and we create them. Every few years we accumulate enough minor changes to create what some futurists call a paradigm shift—a profound change in the way we do things and the way we see the world.

We may be nearing one of those shifts. Call it cocooning, call it burrowing, or call it huddling. Americans are returning to basic values. We have discarded the excesses of the 1980s, adopted the new realities of the 1990s, and rededicated ourselves to the ''important'' things in life.

Evidence of this trend is all around us. People are spending more time at home and are more focused on traditional values. Families and friends are gathering in traditional ways: celebrating holidays and important occasions in family members'

3

lives together. They are also living together in nontraditional ways. The family unit may include "boomerang kids" who have returned home after college or a divorce, elderly parents, or same-sex marriages.

Organized religions continue to have trouble attracting young people in significant numbers, yet people of all ages seem to have a new devotion to spirituality. We've become more accepting of alternative religions and of belief systems that could scarcely be called religions, but attract large numbers of followers. We need to believe in something larger than ourselves, and when we can't find it in one place, we will find it in another.

As I travel around the country giving speeches, conducting seminars, or leading discussion groups about positive thinking and motivation, the one topic that seems to elicit the most response is the subject of spirituality. Senior executives from some of America's best-known corporations come up to me after a seminar and say: "I'm glad you included the mention of spirituality. Most people don't realize how important it is."

I tell these groups at the outset that I am not selling religion. I don't care if you are a Catholic, Protestant, Jew, Muslim, Zen Buddhist, or if you believe in little green men. But, in my experience, the most successful people are those who are anchored to a belief in something larger than themselves.

Our world is changing at such a dizzying pace that we are willing to believe almost anything is possible. Serious, mainstream scientists study UFOs, hold seminars, and exchange information. Supermarket tabloids trumpet Elvis sightings and baby skeletons found on the moon. It is more and more difficult to discern with absolute certainty what is true, what only appears to be true, and what is definitely false.

Our lives are being revolutionized by technology. Although the computer has been around for decades, we are just now beginning to tap its power. I doubt that the most visionary among us could predict how computers will impact our lives in the next few years. John Sculley, the forward thinking CEO of Apple Computer, likens the development of the personal computer to the evolution of the automobile.

In the early days of the automobile, people who drove them were hobbyists, aficionados. They had to understand the inner workings of the engine because if it broke, the owner had to fix it.

There was no infrastructure in place to support this marvelous invention. Roads were poor to nonexistent, and there certainly wasn't a network of service stations, motels, and fast-food restaurants to support a population en route to someplace else.

Today's automobiles are so complicated that a shade tree mechanic of the 1950s couldn't even give one a tune-up. Complex fuel injection systems, electronic ignition systems, anti-lock brakes, and dozens of on-board computers require equally sophisticated test equipment. Yet, when we get into our automobiles, we simply start them up and go, never giving a second thought to the incredibly complex source of power that makes it all possible.

When the computer reaches the level of maturity that automobiles enjoy today, we will have just begun to realize its potential power. Each innovation that simplifies, miniaturizes, and increases the power of the computer moves us closer to the time when anyone can operate one with a minimum of training and virtually no understanding of how it works. And the infrastructure grows with each hardware and software advance.

Our computing power has been multiplied infinitely with the sophistication of the telephone. When AT&T more or less fulfilled its mission to get a single black phone in every home, it began casting about for other applications and innovations. Touch-tone phones in myriad colors were followed by call waiting, call forwarding, cellular phones, and scores of other improvements.

Now, with the vast network of fiber-optic cables and satellites, it is possible to phone virtually any location in the world from wherever you may be. Home computers may be linked by telephone lines to subscription services that offer seemingly endless amounts of data, and in many locations you can do your banking, buy groceries, make airline reservations and pay for your tickets without ever talking to a single person.

The technology already exists for picture phones, and 900 phone numbers allow us to express our opinion about whether or not we believe a potential Supreme Court justice is lying in his Senate confirmation hearings. President Clinton holds "electronic town meetings" in which he talks to us via television and talk show hosts invite us to vote on important issues by telephone.

The combination of phones, computers, and facsimile machines (faxes) has made communication instantaneous around the globe. No longer can oppressive political regimes seize control of the communications media in a coup d'état by taking over the radio and TV stations. China's elderly leaders learned this when they tried to close the country after the June 3–4, 1989, Tiananmen Square demonstrations. They overlooked fax machines. News was faxed in from foreign sympathizers, quickly photocopied and distributed. Often this was the only source of real news inside China.

When we have advanced to the point that all these technologies can be linked—and that day is not far away—we will have truly arrived at the electronic cottage. With computers, phones, and faxes at home, it is no longer necessary to go into the office, save for the socialization we crave, and the consensus building that seems to require face-to-face meetings.

All this technology has created an interesting paradox. Call it the "together but alone" syndrome. Because the government, and everyone who wishes to sell us something, identifies and catalogs us by our income, spending habits, possessions, and where we live, we have become increasingly jealous of our privacy. We interact with others, but we like to conceal our identity. The old-fashioned telephone party line has been replaced by subscription services that allow people to talk about virtually any subject, to be part of a group while protecting their anonymity. Computer networks offer the same flexibility.

The net result is that technology allows us to personalize or generalize as we choose.

Another societal trend that has had and will continue to have a profound influence upon us is decidedly "low-tech" or "no-tech." It is the women's movement. Freed from the shackles of the home, women have moved into the work force and achieved positions of power and influence in business, government, the professions, the arts—in every aspect of society.

In so doing, they have created a "kinder, gentler" workplace less inclined toward ribald jokes and derogatory stereotypes, and they have created new social and economic opportunities and issues. Child care has emerged as a national issue and abortion rights is at the top of every politician's agenda. The demand for convenience products and time-saving services has spawned entire industries that offer help in balancing children, homes, and careers.

Most experts agree that the struggle for women's rights—as with any other minority's rights—won't be over until we truly accept people for what they are without consideration of their gender, race, national origin, or religious preference. I am not so naive as to think this can be achieved overnight, but I firmly believe that as a civilization we cannot begin to approach our vast potential until we stop fighting each other and start working together toward common goals. Indeed, we may ultimately destroy ourselves if we do not do so.

We *can* all succeed together. Only in sports does every winner require a loser. In business, winning creates more opportunity for everyone. Even companies that compete fiercely for market share often expand the entire market for their products. When you become wealthy and successful, you create jobs and opportunities for others. Indeed, the absolute bedrock of civilized society is cooperation for the common good.

In corporate America, far too much time is spent in posturing, outmaneuvering perceived enemies or competitors for a position or title, or generally exercising one's ego. If the time wasted in political gamesmanship could be redirected toward the achievement of mutually-agreed-upon, positive goals, the results would be awe-inspiring. Even in the best-managed companies, far too much time is frittered away with such non-productive activities.

I recognize, of course, that these observations are very subjective. For every belief I've opined here, there are people who vehemently believe—and could advance a persuasive argument—that the opposite is true. The point is this: Ours is a complex, rapidly evolving, confusing time. On this, there is little disagreement.

How do you motivate yourself and others in this far-flung, technologically advanced, complicated and confusing, together-but-alone world in which we live? More than ever we need a firm foundation, the confidence that comes from knowing what we are about, a guiding beacon that helps us steer unerringly toward our goal.

In his book, *Confessions of a Street-Smart Manager*, David

Mahoney writes: "Without a personal philosophy, a strong perception of who you are and what you stand for, you get buffeted around by every person, message, idea and event that comes down the pike. You'll find yourself running off in all directions at once, instead of focusing on the pivotal problems."[1]

If you wish to distinguish yourself in any endeavor, to stand apart from the crowd, you need to establish your own value system. When you know what you are about, you develop the self-confidence that comes with having a purpose for your life. Even more important, having the courage of your convictions allows you to stand firm while others simply drift with the crowd.

A sharply focused philosophy of personal achievement will help sustain you when the going is tough, and it will allow you to reach the highest level of success of which you are capable—personally, professionally, socially, and financially. By studying the principles others have used to achieve incredible success, by examining their lives, we are better able to reach inside ourselves to extract the person we wish to become.

It is an endless process. The human mind is constructed so that when we reach one goal, we quickly set another more difficult one for ourselves. Only when we become complacent do we allow ourselves to rest on our laurels, to revel in past glories. And complacency is quickly followed by dissatisfaction, depression, and failure. We need constant challenge to remain strong.

I hope this book helps you develop a center, a balance in your own life that will provide a springboard to success and help unleash the enormous potential that may now lie dormant within you.

—Samuel A. Cypert

[1]David Mahoney, "Street-Smart Secrets For Success," *Reader's Digest* (August 1988), 64.

1

A Changing World

Well, well—the world must turn upon its axis;
And all mankind turn with it, heads or tails;
And live and die, make love and pay our taxes,
And as the veering wind shifts, shift our sails.

—GEORGE GORDON, LORD BYRON

"This is incredible! It's just incredible; there's no other word to describe it!" On the phone was my friend Karl graf zu Eltz who, among other things, is the proprietor of Burg Eltz, a castle near Koblenz, Germany, that has been in his family since the eleventh century. He and his family have restored the castle and opened it to the public.

I had telephoned him to talk about the Berlin Wall that was being dismantled before our eyes. He on his side of the Atlantic and I on mine watched in utter fascination as on live television people from East and West Germany tossed bouquets of flowers over the wall and drank champagne toasts in an all-night party celebrating the forthcoming reunification of the two Germanys.

As we and millions of others around the world literally watched history being made, it was with a sense of jubilation slightly tempered with apprehension—apprehension because from this day forward, the world would never be the same.

Both Karl and I had grown up with the wall. It had existed as a world symbol of the cold war, the iron curtain, the opposing philosophies of government that we supposed would always be at odds. And while the wall symbolized oppression, it also symbolized permanence. Now, it would be gone. What would it leave in its wake?

In the few short years since that momentous event, we have seen a failed revolution in China and a failed coup in the Soviet Union quickly followed by a new social order and the dissolution of the Communist regime. At this writing, the fragile Russian Federation and its disparate, contentious assortment of republics seem perilously close to yet another upheaval.

In Iraq, we fought one of the shortest, deadliest wars in history—live on television. My wife, Merrilee, gave birth to our son, Joseph, as CNN's Chuck Jaco gave a live update from Saudi Arabia, an incident that elicited a chuckle from Jaco when she told him about it on a call-in program after the war was over. Our story was one of the millions of everyday things that occurred as momentous world events swirled about us.

Change Is Ubiquitous

Changes large and small are all around us. The relentless march of the Information Age brings us news of a turbulent world, and it increasingly affects every aspect of our everyday lives. Desktop computers are commonplace in the office of today's executive, and factory workers run computer-controlled machines and sophisticated robotics equipment that perform tasks that formerly could be done only by human beings. Home computers—with a little help from a thinking person—do everything from making coffee to paying bills.

Our social fabric is severely strained and occasionally rent by quick, violent, unanticipated events. I had a sense of *déjà vu*—that once again events were out of the control of any individual or institution—when my friend Joseph Ruggiero phoned and apologized for not returning my call of the day before. He'd been evacuated from his Beverly Hills office because of the riots in Los Angeles.

The riots, which caused hundreds of millions of dollars in damage, followed the acquittal of four white policemen accused of using excessive force in the arrest of black motorist Rodney King. Because the event had been videotaped by a bystander, all the world watched as the cops applied their nightsticks to King. Whatever the jury said, they had already been convicted in the court of public opinion.

Coping Begins with Acceptance

How does one cope with change on such a massive scale? It begins with acceptance. It was the first century Roman philosopher Pliny the Elder who first observed that the only permanent thing in life is change, yet we continue to resist it, somehow believing that if we don't accept change, it won't happen.

In his watershed book, *Future Shock*, best-selling author Alvin Toffler pointed out that today's frenetic pace of change no longer allows us the luxury of gradually, unconsciously, "organically" adapting to change. Instead of resisting change, we have to learn to welcome and manage it. We must master evolution; we must shape our own tomorrows. We must "anticipate and design the future."[1]

The future belongs to those who not only accept change, but embrace it, enjoy it, and use it to their advantage. These days, it isn't even enough to be able to cope with change. We need to anticipate it and plan our response to changes going on around us if we are to remain competitive at what we do. We can't completely control change, but we can anticipate it and control our participation in it and our reaction to it.

Our new attitude must be: change is good! And we must sell this idea to our employees, our customers, and everyone around us. Change management consultant Darryl Connor, who heads up Atlanta-based Organizational Design Resources (ODR), tells clients and seminar participants that as long as the present or anticipated pain of changing things is greater than the pain of the present situation, people are reluctant to change. A manager's or leader's job is to help others feel the pain of not changing.

---

[1] Alvin Toffler, *Future Shock* (New York: Bantam Books, published by arrangement with Random House, 1970), 485.

Connor also emphasizes the importance of timing. He uses the analogy of an ice cube to illustrate the point. If an ice cube is frozen in the familiar rectangular shape and we would like to reshape it into a triangle, for example, there are two ways to go about it. We can either thaw the ice cube and refreeze it in the shape of a triangle, or we can smash it to bits with a hammer and re-form it. The thawing and refreezing option will form a stronger, more cohesive unit, but smashing and re-forming is faster. There is a time and place for each.

If you find yourself in a situation where such things are going on around you, you may or may not be able to influence the outcome. But, you can always influence your reaction to it. If the company for which you work is undergoing rapid change—and most do with regularity—you have several choices: You can resist change, you can ignore it, you can encourage it, or you can find another job. Each action has consequences.

Anticipating Change and Profiting from It

Change affects us all, whether we are management consultants, work in a large corporation, or run a fast-food restaurant. One of Weatherford, Oklahoma's leading citizens when I attended college there in the mid-1960s was Al Belanger. Belanger ran a favorite hangout of the college students. He was friendly, served good pizza and cold draft beer—and his restaurant was across the street from the campus.

He also ran an A & W restaurant on Route 66, which ran through the center of town. At the time, Route 66 was the best way to travel west; America passed through Weatherford on its way somewhere else. Belanger sold motorists hamburgers and hot dogs. Times were good and business prospered.

In the midst of all this economic bliss, however, there was a small dark cloud on the horizon in the form of Interstate 40, which was under construction at the time. I-40 would replace U.S. 66 and bypass the town. Business people in town speculated about the changes the new highway would bring and debated its effect on the local economy. Merchants considered roadside signs and special promotions to keep the tourists coming through Weatherford. While some of the others considered their options, Belanger bought a plot of land near the interstate and began construction of a new A & W restaurant.

I've long since lost track of him, but I'd bet a cheeseburger and a root beer float that Al Belanger is somewhere out there serving fast-food to America and doing quite well financially. He accepted change as an inevitable fact of life and chose to participate constructively in it.

Much of Belanger's success in anticipating change was the result of his obsessive focus on customers long before it became the technique *du jour* in modern management. He knew his customers and what they wanted because he was a hands-on manager. He was there every day talking to them, serving them, and making sure that they were happy.

Know Your Customers

Belanger didn't have to hire outside consultants or require weekly progress reports from several layers of managers to figure out that travelers unfamiliar with the terrain would be reluctant to exit the interstate to search for a restaurant. They wanted to see the sign and the interstate exit and entrance. Al knew this because he asked his customers questions and they told him the answers.

Whatever line of business you are in or whatever your position is within your company, this rule applies: know your customers. You can't help them solve their problems if you don't know and understand their concerns. Conversely, if you know how they think and the worries that keep them awake at night, you can make a lot of money selling them the products and services that bring them peace of mind.

Baby Boomers' Influence

A single group that has precipitated more change than any other in the U.S will soon have yet another profound effect upon our lives. That group is now going through its mid-life crisis. The reference, of course, is to the baby boomers, the first wave of which will be fifty years of age in 1996.

Because of its sheer size, the baby boom generation set the national agenda as it moved through the stages of life. When they were young, back in the 1960s, the emphasis was on youth, fast cars, and music. As they built their careers in the seventies and eighties, the focus was on greed. Once again, we are seeing our priorities shifted to suit their needs and interests. As baby boomers become more conservative in middle age, we see renewed focus on basic values—home and family.[2]

They are also shifting career priorities. As they begin to come to grips with the fact that not everyone can (or is willing to pay the price to) be chief executive officer of the company and begin to plateau in their careers, they are affecting the way they and others work. They want more balance in their lives, and if they don't find total fulfillment in their careers, they will find it in other interests. Be prepared: If history is any indicator, their priorities will become our priorities.

Many of today's leading social issues—health care, education, child care, and urban problems—are driven by this large population segment's social conscience balanced against its own selfish interests.

Such information may be of little more than passing interest until you consider its implications. Many successful careers have been built by catering to this demographic bulge, and there are plenty of opportunities ahead. As the post–WW II generation ages and its interests change, members of this group will become big buyers of timesaving and leisure time products. They are also likely to increase their savings and investments as they begin to think about retirement, and they stand to inherit a great deal of wealth from their elderly parents. Great opportunities await those who anticipate and respond to the baby boomers' needs and desires.

Changing Workplace Values

This disproportionately large generation will also influence the workplace. As the boomers assume a larger and larger role in business management, they will bring their values with them. Workers will be less interested in traditional motivators, and demographic shifts, attitude changes, intensified worldwide competition, and a shrinking economy that is reshaping itself to cope with the Information Age will probably combine

---

[2]Robert H. Schirmer, *The New Demographics*, a speech to building industry analysts at a Masco Corporation presentation in Las Vegas, May 1992.

to further limit our ability to motivate workers with customary raises and promotions.

Managers will have to find new incentives such as compensation packages that include profit participation or some form of ownership in the company. Our challenge will be to link pay more closely with performance and cope with a work force that is highly mobile and has little loyalty to any particular company or industry.

Population Shifts

There is another fundamental change under way in the U.S. that will have a profound influence on the way we work: Since the 1960s, the population growth rate has declined while life expectancy has increased. The result is fewer young people entering the work force and oldsters staying longer and in some cases starting second careers after retirement. Companies have had to adapt. When McDonald's couldn't recruit enough teenagers to serve Big Macs and fries, it turned to older people who wanted to earn extra cash to supplement their income and add a little purpose to their lives.

It seemed strange at first to be greeted by a senior citizen in a McDonald's uniform, but now they have become a part of the landscape. Older and younger people work side by side in restaurants across the country. It's a good thing for both groups; they learn from each other, and, hopefully, they become more tolerant of other points of view.

The effects of the shrinking birthrate on the work force have to a degree been masked by other societal changes going on. Women and minorities have moved in to fill the vacuum, although there are some early indications that both the birthrate and the number of women in the work force may be changing.

Putting Careers on Hold

Reports are beginning to surface that more and more women are putting their careers on hold to stay home and raise the kids. In 1992, the Bureau of Labor Statistics reported the first decline in the women's work force in twenty-five years. Because the decline was concentrated in the 25–39 age group, the bureau attributed it in part to an increased birthrate. Of course, one statistical bulge is as likely to be an aberration as the beginning of a trend, but pollsters report that fifty-six percent of women who responded to a recent survey said they would consider giving up their careers outside the home if they could afford it.[3]

If the parents of young children decide it is more important for one of them to stay home with the children than to buy a BMW, new workers will have to be found and trained. "And given the dearth of skilled labor at a time when the fastest growing occupations will require the most preparation, industry's ability to develop training programs will be the key factor impacting both the nation's economic health and individual career advancement in the years ahead," says *Black Enterprise* magazine.[4]

One positive benefit that might result from these changes may be that Americans finally come to realize that we need each other. We may be forced to respect each other as individuals—without regard for our color, gender, or religious beliefs. Because we must depend on each other economically, perhaps we will learn to work together to solve our social problems.

Succeeding in the New Order

To succeed in the new order, we must all become more diplomatic and more sensitive to ethnic and social variety. We will have to focus more on the things that unite us as employees of the same company, members of the same union or profession, or other shared interests, and to de-emphasize the characteristics we possess that may tend to divide us.

Managers will have to find new ways to motivate workers. Flex time, shared positions, day-care centers at the office, working at home, and more leisure time are but a few of the possibilities.

This is not altogether new. Managers have always had limits on salary budgets. Businesses cannot remain competitive if

---

[3]Ann Sweeney and Dwight E. M. Angell, "Women Trade Money for 'Mommy,'" *Detroit News*, 10 May 1992, 1A, 13A.
[4]Adrienne S. Harris, "And the Prepared Will Inherit the Future," *Black Enterprise* (February 1990), 121–128.

they pay their workers significantly more than the competition; such costs are built into the cost of products and services. If the price rises too much, consumers won't buy.

In any event, most research shows that money ceases to be a motivator after we reach a certain comfort level—unless it is in amounts significant enough to change our life-style. Even then, we very quickly adapt to new income levels and motivation based on a big raise alone soon fades. We have always had to find creative ways to challenge ourselves and others with whom we work or those we manage.

The Power of Information

Properly used, information can be a powerful motivator in a world of change, and today, there is no shortage of information about any subject we can imagine. The trick is not to find the data in our information-intensive world; the difficulty lies in sorting it and figuring out what it means to us.

Keeping up requires constant reading and studying. Self-improvement should be part of our daily routine. Choose a time of the day that is best for you, when you are relaxed, there are no distractions, and you have the time to devote your full attention to reading and thinking. Your daily ritual should include setting aside time—preferably the same time every day—to read the newspaper, a trade magazine, or a good book. Seek variety in your reading. Whatever you read will help expand your mind. Make notes, save clippings, and train yourself to retain information that is of value to you.

Use technology to your advantage. Watch training or motivational films and videos, and listen to audiocassettes. As you study, watch for the unusual, the anomalies, the things that surprise you in light of everything you already know. Look for emerging patterns, events that affect more than one industry or geographic region of the country. A new idea or fad is well on its way to becoming a trend when it begins to cross industry or geographic lines, and recognition of it as such can create great opportunities. W. Clement Stone labeled the technique the R2A2 principle: recognize, relate, assimilate, and apply information from any field that will help you in the achievement of your goals, whatever they may be.

Capitalizing on Change: The Prodigy Story

Recognizing changes in the external environment allows us to adapt our behavior to take advantage of situations and opportunities when they occur. One great example of a group that capitalized on an emerging trend was the organizers of the Prodigy interactive personal computer service.

A joint venture between Sears and IBM, Prodigy filled a gap in home computer service. As personal computers proliferated and users learned how to operate them effectively, they sought new services. They bought modems and transmitted messages to each other, and subscribed to various individual data bases, but there was no single source for a wide variety of services.

Enter Prodigy. The purchase of the service includes a one-time fee that covers the cost of the software, instruction manuals, and a compact Hayes modem designed for personal use. Everything consumers need to link up with the outside world is included in the package. As part of the agreement, subscribers agree to pay a small monthly fee for the service.

Once the software is installed and the system connected to a telephone line, on command the computer dials a local telephone number to connect to the Prodigy service. The service allows users to make travel arrangements through a travel agency connected with Prodigy, send electronic messages to other members, play games, shop, do their banking, buy and sell stocks, access an on-line encyclopedia, and receive news, weather, and sports bulletins. All of these activities can be done from home at any time of the day or night.

Neither IBM, Sears, nor Prodigy invented the personal computer. The originators of the Prodigy service merely recognized a trend and capitalized on it by pulling together a variety of services and making them available to consumers for their use—at their convenience. Today, there are some 1.75 million individual subscribers to the Prodigy service and 150 businesses that sell their goods and services to them.

Softening the Impact of Change

Anticipating trends and preparing for them also have the effect of softening their impact upon us personally. If we watch trends develop and take an interest in them, we are more inclined to accept them and use them to our advantage.

To do so, we have first to accept the notion that learning is a process that continues throughout our lifetimes, not something that is finished when we have become "educated" and graduate from school. To be successful in the future will require intimate knowledge of aspects of science and technology that we can't even imagine today.

Take advantage of information that is readily available to help you stay current in your field. If you supervise others, reward superior performers with training, attendance at seminars, reimbursement for college courses, and the like. As the world continues its rapid pace of change, learning will become an essential part of the job, and continuing education will be part of every company's daily routine.

Experts estimate that by the year 2000, seventy-five percent of all workers currently employed will need retraining to keep their jobs.[5] As individuals and as companies, we can expect to spend substantial sums on training during the next few years.

As workers become better educated and more skilled, other adjustments will follow. They will insist upon participating in decisions that affect their lives and careers. The best managers and leaders will be those who seize every opportunity to get people involved. Active participation in planning and decision-making gives us ownership. We are more interested in the outcome.

Preparing Ourselves and Others for Change

Making people feel good about themselves and their contribution will be an important part of a manager's job. Respecting workers' opinions and involving them—individually or in problem-anticipation and problem-solving groups, advisory committees, quality circles, and discussion groups—will become increasingly important in a work environment that demands interdependence and cooperation between groups of culturally diverse coworkers.

It's like flying a jumbo jet. The captain is in charge, but he

---

[5]Harris, 121–128.

can't do the flight engineer's job, nor the navigator's, nor the flight attendants'. He must depend on the specialists in each area to do the job they are trained to do. Only then will the passengers arrive safely, on time, well fed, and happy.

There is a lesson in that analogy for all of us as we move toward an increasingly technology-driven society.

Key Points and Action Items

1. Coping with change begins with acceptance. The world will change whether we like it or not. If we adjust our attitudes and recognize the opportunities inherent in change, we can profit from them.

2. Know your customers. Talk to them and determine their needs and desires. Sell value-added solutions that give them peace of mind.

3. Watch the baby boomers. Because their generation is disproportionately large, they drive many of the changes in our society.

4. Pay attention to trends. Read and study constantly to keep up with what is going on in your business, trade, or profession. In the new order of things, learning will be a lifelong commitment.

5. Be prepared for more changes ahead. Be flexible and learn to be more tolerant of other points of view as we become a more culturally diverse country.

2

Success Defined

*If a man goes into business with only the idea
of making money, the chances are he won't.*

—JOYCE CLYDE HALL

The air traffic controller advised Captain Al Haynes that all
the runways at the Sioux City airport had been cleared for the
emergency landing of United Flight 242.

At the controls of the DC-10, Haynes responded genially,
"You want to be particular and make it a runway, huh? I'm
just aiming for Iowa."

What followed was one of the most amazing feats in aviation history. Flight 242 was en route from Denver to Chicago
with 296 passengers on board when one of the plane's engines
exploded. The force of the blast and the shrapnel from the
explosion severed the plane's hydraulic lines, disabling the
steering and control systems.

With remarkable skill and daring, Haynes, copilot Bill Records, and flight engineer Dudley Dvorak fashioned a plan to
land the craft, a plan that later could not be duplicated by
seasoned veterans in forty-five simulated attempts. They
would steer the plane by varying the thrust of the two remaining engines.

Miraculously, they were able to get the plane to Sioux City

for a crash landing. Because he couldn't slow the DC-10, it bounced, cartwheeled, and exploded into flame, killing 112 people. But 184 survived almost certain death as a result of Haynes's success.[1]

Success Redefined

The moment that engine exploded, Haynes's definition of success changed radically. His only goal, one that he focused upon with calm intensity, was to get the crippled aircraft to the ground without killing himself, his crew, and his passengers.

Hopefully, most of us will never know the intensity of desire or the adrenaline rush Captain Haynes must have experienced in that hour of crisis, yet every day, every week, every year throughout our lives, we too adjust our definition of success. Often, we can identify particular events that were turning points in our lives, times that from that day forward we did things differently.

Building on Small Successes

Most major goals, however, are not reached in a blaze of glory, in a single moment of truth. Instead, they are reached after we've tried many things; some worked, some didn't. If we fail, we learn from our mistakes, correct our course, and try again. Big successes usually follow a long series of small, cumulative successes.

It's similar to flying a plane or steering a ship. What may appear on a navigator's chart to be a straight line from Point A to Point B is in truth a series of small zigzag lines. The pilot must constantly adjust to compensate for wind shifts, variations in the earth's magnetic field, and other traffic in the area, some of which is headed for the same destination.

Plateau Thinking

Pat Ryan, CEO of Aon Corporation, the giant multinational insurance company, encourages what he calls plateau thinking.

---

[1] "Wind Beneath Their Wings," *People* (February 24, 1992), 84–86.

"I believe that at each new level of achievement you have to push yourself or you'll retrench. So I'm a great advocate of reach one plateau, then springing to another, and so on. When you do, your capacity as a person is expanded.

"Success is stretching to reach your goal, then never being satisfied," Ryan says. "You can't conceive how far up is, except for the limitations of your own mind. That may not be very good English, but all I really mean is that once you decide how high it is that you want to go, that's as far as you will go."

With Ryan as with many others who have achieved notable financial and business success, the concept of success is ever changing. When we reach one goal we have set for ourselves, we immediately set another, bigger one. It's part of human nature.

Happiness Is Hard Work

Says University of Chicago psychology professor Mihaly Csikszentmihalyi, "People are happiest not when they are 'having fun' but when they're striving to achieve goals they have set for themselves. In short, happiness is often hard work."

When we are feeling overworked, it may be difficult to believe that we are happiest when we are working our hardest, but neither would we accept the notion that we would be permanently satisfied if life were one continuous day at the beach. After studying the subject for twenty-five years, Csikszentmihalyi concluded that the experiences we recall as the happiest of our lives occurred when we were so absorbed in what we were doing that we forgot about everything else.

There is something inside ourselves that makes us feel unfulfilled unless we are challenged. If work has become routine and boring, look for new ways to perform tedious tasks. Compete against yourself to improve your productivity. Use the time you save to learn something new and different.

Develop outside interests. When you look forward to participating in a community event or learning to play a musical instrument, mundane chores become more bearable. Happiness is never awarded to you—it must be earned. Don't resent others for what they have or dream about things that you believe would make you happy. Happiness can only come from within, and you must create it.

Live in the Moment

Csikszentmihalyi's advice: "Pay attention to what you're doing in each moment. Enjoy your skills as you move from day to day, and become more in touch with your own potential. Don't let your mind be led from the outside, by commercials or easy answers from self-help books. Realize that life is difficult but it's in your hands, and you can make it into what you want."[2]

We all have differing levels of competence and of aspirations. We can't all be CEO of the company, a famous rock star, or an Olympic runner. But, in the diversity of our personalities and our capabilities is the very essence of what makes us alike—and what makes us different.

Our objective for our lives and the goals we set for ourselves along the way may be vastly different, but we share one trait that is as old as life itself. We all want to improve, to be better at what we do. We quickly become bored with doing the same thing over and over.

Find New Outlets

People who work in repetitive jobs, or for managers who don't challenge them, find other outlets for their unused potential. They are leaders in church, school, or civic affairs or they are part-time painters or musicians. Often, their managers and coworkers have no idea about the responsible positions these people hold outside of work.

To help break the ice in company-sponsored workshops and seminars, I frequently ask participants to get acquainted with a person in the group that they don't normally work with, then introduce the person to the group. They can use any speaking style they wish, or they may tell us anything about the person that the individual is willing to share.

The only criterion is: make that person interesting to the

[2]Judy Woodburn, "What Makes Us Happy?" *Special Report* (January/February 1992), 13–15.

rest of the group. Tell us something different or unusual about him or her. Don't tell us their titles or positions; we already know all that. Tell us something about the person.

There is always a surprise or two when people reveal their personal achievements to people with whom they do not normally talk about such things. It electrifies the entire group on those occasions when, for example, an executive realizes that a secretary (whom he has for years treated like a child) in her spare time has a responsible position on a board of directors or is active in a civic group charged with the oversight of a large organization. Ordinary people do amazing things when they are allowed to do so.

Philosophers have for years debated whether great events make great people or if ordinary people rise to greatness when the situation demands it. There may be some truth to both theories, but time and time again when we see people on the evening news who have just risked their lives to save someone else's, they say, "It was nothing that anyone else wouldn't have done under the circumstances." Perhaps that's their way of saying that we all have within us the potential for greatness, but we don't challenge ourselves as we should. It takes an unexpected event or crisis to demand that we face up to our potential.

Be Your Best—for Yourself

Those who rise to the top of any sport, any profession, or any vocation are those who motivate themselves to be the best they can be—for themselves. They don't need any external stimuli or a supervisor or coach looking over their shoulders to encourage them. They are tougher on themselves than anyone else could ever be.

Unfortunately, in our culture we learn early on that it's not good to be different. The message may be subtle or it may be overt, but it is clear that to be a part of the group, you can't stand out from the crowd. In school, those who excel are taunted by others. Every generation has its own labels, but whether they are eggheads, dorks, or dweebs, they are the guys who grow up to be Bill Gates, founder and CEO of Microsoft and a multimillionaire before he was out of his twenties.

We also love to see others fail. We build giant pedestals

upon which to place public heroes, then chip away at the pedestal until we destroy them. It gives us enormous satisfaction to see that they are ordinary people who have the same foibles and frailties that we do. We overlook their achievements in order to focus on their weaknesses, somehow believing that doing so makes us more equal.

Because our lessons about competition are learned in sports and in school, we believe that in order for one to succeed, someone else must fail. It is win or lose. We often carry that erroneous assumption with us all our lives, when in actual fact the exact opposite is true. We can succeed together. A manager who drives himself hard and succeeds creates opportunities for others. As he is promoted, so are his people. An entrepreneur who builds a dynamic and successful business creates jobs for many and growth opportunities for his best employees.

The first step in achieving success—at anything—is to discard much of what you have learned and realize that for most of us, achievement in any field means working harder and doing better than our peers while simultaneously helping them become the best they can be. Success is both cooperative and exclusive. We all need others to help us achieve our personal goals, and to get them to help us, we have to give something of equal value in return.

Of course, for a time you can exploit others for your personal gain. Many people are generous and giving, and they enjoy helping others. But, if you never give anything in return, even the kindest and most generous will eventually tire of a one-sided relationship. There is a price tag attached to success at every level.

You Can Have Anything but You Can't Have Everything

Several years ago, I had the opportunity to meet the great Earl Nightingale, whose radio broadcasts and recordings have inspired millions of listeners over the years. Although he was getting on in years and in poor health at the time, he still had the magic. I've never forgotten his words that day, delivered in his own inimitable style and voice. He said: ''There is nothing in this world that you cannot have in five years' time if you are willing to pay the price for it. Think about it. Anything you want can be yours in just five years if you are willing to do what's necessary to get it.''

If you imagine yourself in the house of your dreams or at the controls of your own airplane, you can have either. As you read these words, you know you can have them. Already you are thinking of what you would have to give up and the steps you would have to take to achieve those goals. You would have to save enough for a down payment, maintain a good credit rating, cut back on other expenses, make more money, get a pilot's license . . . but all of those things are possible and ''do-able'' if that's the thing you want more than anything else in the world.

The difficulty lies not in achieving a goal once you've set it for yourself; the difficulty lies in deciding which goal is more important. We are all faced with an endless array of needs and wants, most of which are attainable. However, it is not likely that they are all attainable at the same time. Success requires focus, priorities, and determination bordering on obsession.

A World-Class Competitor

There is perhaps no better example of the character and obsessive focus on a goal than that of Olympic athletes. For years, they train endlessly to earn the right to compete against others with similar abilities and training until they become the best in the country. They are then rewarded by being allowed to train even harder so they can compete with the best in the world.

In an essay on the Olympics, award-winning filmmaker and sports historian Bud Greenspan recalled the story of John Stephen Akhwari, a marathon runner who in the 1968 Olympics in Mexico City received a standing ovation from the spectators for finishing *last* in the race. He had severely injured his knee in a fall, and it was bloodied and bandaged as he hobbled around the track toward the finish line.

When he was asked why, since he was in obvious pain and had no chance of winning a medal, had he not quit, Akhwari replied with simple eloquence: ''My country did not send me 7,000 miles to start the race. They sent me 7,000 miles to FINISH the race.''

The young runner was driven by his own desire and "inspired by the words that have sent Olympians into the arena for more than two thousand years—from the earliest days in ancient Greece:

> *Ask not alone for victory, ask for*
> *courage, for if you can endure, you*
> *bring honor to yourself. Even more,*
> *you bring honor to us all."* [3]

The Importance of Balance

Success is about doing your best; it's about constant course correction, reaching one plateau and springing to another; and it's about working with others to your mutual advantage. But it's more than these things. Success is also about balance.

We Americans are an impatient lot. We want money, influence, and power—the traditional components of success—but we are not willing to wait until we reach the top to enjoy the perks. We want a good income and the time to enjoy it. We believe we can build companies and create jobs without destroying the environment and at the same time help those who are less fortunate than we are.

Having it all means having a fulfilling career without neglecting everything else that is important. Part of the process of refining and adjusting our goals means that at various times of our lives we have to devote more time to one aspect or another. Early in our careers, for example, we are building. We work long hours and put in the extra effort to earn promotions or to build a clientele or a business. The focus is on money and careers.

Problems develop when we become so obsessed with any one aspect of our lives that we neglect other important parts of it. When we become unbalanced in one part of our lives the imbalance negatively affects our entire life. If we wreck our family relationships or lose all our friends because we

---

[3] Bud Greenspan, "Olympic," *Lands' End* catalog (Early June 1992), 39–41.

spend every waking moment working or worrying about work, we are unsuccessful at both work and in relationships.

A Changing View of Success

The way we view success is changing. As corporations flatten their hierarchies and fewer middle managers are required to supervise today's "knowledge workers," a movement is beginning to reward employees based on their knowledge and skill, rather than on their power or number of people they manage. In the future, careers may be built more on horizontal moves rather than the traditional vertical climb toward the top of the corporate ladder.

This approach gained momentum when boards of directors and the Securities and Exchange Commission began to design executive compensation schemes that more closely link pay to performance and worked its way through the rest of the organization. The idea goes by various names, "pay for skills," "skill-based pay," or "knowledge based compensation."

Whatever it's called, the goal is to pay people based on their ability to contribute and to continue to learn so they can contribute even more. " 'Pay-for-skills' values learning instead of control," said Marc Sternfeld, a managing director at Salomon Brothers, which is instituting such a system at a new facility in Tampa that will handle much of the investment banking firm's back office paperwork.

If it is successful, Salomon's new approach may redirect the career paths of employees. Instead of being penalized for making horizontal moves, they will be encouraged to gain knowledge and acquire expertise in a variety of subjects in order to advance in the company. Their pay and promotions will be based upon their success in playing by this new set of rules.

Creating New Paradigms

Salomon's plan is breaking many of the old paradigms and establishing new ones. Instead of transferring a cadre of people to staff the Tampa operation, the firm is hiring new people who have no experience in the brokerage business—and thus no preconceived notions about the way things should work.

Replacing the 135 managers, who supervised 670 employees in New York, will be 17 "coaches" advising 500 team members.

Teams will be formed around product areas such as foreign exchange or corporate bonds instead of traditional functional areas of expertise such as accounting or data processing. Team members will be paid on their ability to complete assignments and on their ability to learn more about the firm's products. Both management and other members of the team will influence pay raises; no longer will satisfying the boss be enough to merit a raise. If the plan works the way Salomon Brothers hopes it will, the firm expects that team members will eventually earn more than their coaches.[4]

The investment bankers will then be faced with the same challenges professional sports team coaches have wrestled with for years: how to manage a group of well-paid, highly motivated, competitive, individual achievers who are difficult to replace—and they know it. Dealing with such challenges will become commonplace as work becomes increasingly specialized and technical.

A Look at the Past and at the Future

Not long ago, I had the opportunity to visit the studios of WBBM-TV, the CBS affiliate in Chicago, and the CNN studios in Atlanta. The visits occurred within a few days of each other, which served to intensify the impressions of each.

The CBS studio was the one from which the historic John Kennedy/Richard Nixon debates were broadcast. It was much as you would expect a broadcast studio to be: a dark monolithic structure filled with television paraphernalia—cameras, cables, lighting equipment, and the like.

The CNN studios, on the other hand, were more like a computer store than the home of a television network. The well-lighted newsroom had circular work modules, each with several computer terminals. The center of each module was slightly elevated and also had a computer terminal that allowed

---

[4]Andrea Gabor, "After the Pay Revolution, Job Titles Won't Matter," *New York Times,* 17 May 1992, Sec. 3–5.

the supervisor of the group to review and edit the work his or her team produced. Graphics and text created by workers at the terminals eventually worked their way to the nearby enclosed studio where on-air personalities read the news that was broadcast to viewers around the world.

It struck me at the time that I had just seen the television news workplace of the past—and the one of the future.

Has our ability to harness technology had the expected effect of improving our standard of living and the quality of our lives? Probably not. It seems quaint today that we once worried about what we would do with the abundance of leisure time that our technologically advanced timesaving devices would create. We needn't have worried; excess leisure time never reached crisis proportions.

Harvard economist Juliet B. Schor estimates that Americans on average work some 163 hours more than we did twenty years ago. We're still way behind the Japanese who work about a half hour a day longer than we do, but the French and Germans work 320 hours less than we do with no apparent loss of efficiency.

The result, according to Schor, is that we've become "a nation of stressed-out workers and neglected children, and millions of unemployed or underemployed people who could be sharing the burden if someone would hire them." She reminds us that "wanting more time off isn't a sign of national decay. Spare time is supposed to be one of the benefits of living in a technological culture," she says.[5]

Around the world, people are seeking balance in their lives. We want the security that comes from financial success, but we also want the satisfaction that comes only from knowing we did our best, that we were challenged and we rose to the challenge, whether there was money involved or not. We also want the respect of our peers, the love of our families, and the pride that comes from the knowledge that we made a difference, that the world was a tiny bit better as a result of our having been a part of it.

---

[5]Hiawatha Bray, "All Work, Little Play," a review of *The Overworked American: The Unexpected Decline of Leisure* by Juliet B. Schor, *Detroit Free Press*, 23 February 1992, D–1.

One Man's Odyssey

In his biography, *Odyssey*, Apple Computer CEO John Sculley tells about how he agonized over his decision to leave Pepsi and join the rapidly growing computer company. For some time, his friend and Apple cofounder, Steve Jobs, had attempted to persuade him to leave a fairly secure and promising career with the soft drink and snack food giant and cast his lot with Apple, a company with a decidedly less certain future.

As they talked, Sculley weighed the pros and cons and struggled to decide what he should do. Finally, Jobs turned to his friend and said quietly, "Do you want to spend the rest of your life selling sugared water, or do you want a chance to change the world?"[6]

For Sculley, that one statement crystallized the question, and haunted him for days afterward. He took the job.

Success Is Relative, Individual, and Personal

Success has been defined as many things, but it still comes down to this: Success is relative, and it's individual and personal. It is relative because it is never reached. The moment we reach a goal, we must replace it with another or we begin to atrophy. As we become better and more skilled at what we do, our goals expand accordingly.

It's individual because we all have different capabilities. Success isn't all genetic; great athletes don't always become world-class competitors only because they come from a better gene pool. If that were the case, someone would figure out how to manipulate the genetics and breed them. They become great athletes by building on their natural abilities by endless training and conditioning. The same is true with musicians, dancers, or those in any other field where success is measured by individual performance.

Success is also characterized by persistence. Popular folklore is filled with stories of those who succeeded because they

---

[6]John Sculley with John A. Byrne, *Odyssey* (New York: Harper and Row, 1987), 90.

had the courage of their convictions and persisted until they were eventually recognized for their achievements.

Unfortunately, the reverse is also true. There are an equal number of tales about those who gave up just before they reached success. They sold the claim to someone else who struck gold just a few feet beyond where they quit digging.

Success almost always involves working harder and smarter than everyone else. It means starting work a half hour early in order to get a head start, and it often means staying late to finish up a project or plan for tomorrow. It means training harder and learning more so you will be more valuable to your team or your organization.

That's where the personal part of success comes in. You alone can decide what the right balance is for your life, the price you are willing to pay to get what you want from life. Everything comes at a cost. You pay for money with your time, but if you like what you do enough, if your drive comes from within, not as a result of external pressures to do better, to earn more, work becomes fun.

Perhaps the best definition of success comes from Beverly Hills, Michigan, resident George Giffen, vice president of marketing for Colorama, Limited. At a recent motivational seminar sponsored by my favorite Borders bookstore, he volunteered this: "Success is when you can't tell whether you are working or playing."

Key Points and Action Items

1. The definition of success changes constantly. When we reach one goal we have set for ourselves, we automatically raise our sights. It's human nature.

2. Happines is hard work. No one can create it for you; it can only come from within. If you are bored or restless, find new creative outlets for unused potential. Take a night course or learn to play the banjo.

3. You can have anything you want in five years' time. You just can't have everything you want. All success comes with a price tag attached. You must give up some things to gain others.

4. Success is about balance. When we become so obsessed with any one aspect of our lives that we neglect others, the imbalance affects our entire life.

5. We are all different with different capabilities, goals, and desires. We can become outstanding at what we do only through endless learning and conditioning.

3

What Is a Family?

*The family is the miniature commonwealth
upon whose integrity the safety of the larger
commonwealth depends.*

—FELIX ADLER

As the presidential campaign heated up in the summer of 1992, the issue of family values reached center stage in a most peculiar way. In a flap that elevated the ridiculous to sublime heights, the vice president of the U.S. assailed the fictitious sitcom character "Murphy Brown" for "mocking the importance of fathers by bearing a child alone."

The popular Monday night program had ended its season with the show's namesake giving birth to a child out of wedlock. The very next day, in a speech televised from San Francisco, Vice President Dan Quayle chastised Murphy Brown for her "poverty of values," implying that somehow she and her kind were responsible for the disintegration of the family in America.

The White House issued statements, changed its mind, issued more statements, and provided newspaper pundits with column fodder for years to come. George Bush waffled and tried to stay out of it—unsuccessfully—and his spokesman, Marlin Fitzwater, after several futile attempts to put a politically correct spin on the story, gave up and offered to marry Murphy Brown. The difficulty with that idea, of course, was that while the fictional character was single, Candice Bergen, who played Brown in the show, wasn't.

Sensing an important "photo op," President Clinton, then the Democratic challenger, leaped into the fray, coming down on the side of God, motherhood, and apple pie. Independent candidate H. Ross Perot called the whole thing "goofy," but, before the flap was over, set off a media frenzy of his own when he told ABC's Barbara Walters that he would not allow gays in sensitive positions in his cabinet, and that he wouldn't hire adulterers at all. "I put a very strong store on strong moral values," he said.

Headline writers had a field day; the *New York Daily News* trumpeted: "Quayle to Murphy Brown: YOU TRAMP!" Foreigners (who often find Americans baffling) watched in utter disbelief.

The magazine *Entertainment Weekly* released a poll of six hundred Americans that revealed the majority of them believed that Murphy Brown would be a better parent and a better president than Dan Quayle. In parenting, the score was Brown forty-three percent to Quayle thirty-eight percent; in government, it was Brown forty percent, Quayle thirty-eight percent. The balance of those surveyed—perhaps the most sensible of the lot—refused to answer the questions.

Conflicting Values

The media chewed on the topic for weeks. Boston *Globe* columnist Ellen Goodman chastised Vice President Quayle for, among other things, lumping single mothers into one category that made no distinction between a high school sophomore with a part-time job at McDonald's and a successful, mature, career woman. In Goodman's view, Quayle overlooked the substantial difference in the ability of each to handle the dual challenges of parenting and a career.

The way Goodman saw it, the problem is not that we have a "poverty of values." The problem is that "we have a plethora of values, most of them in conflict with each other.''[1] In our complicated world, we often attempt to reconcile contradictory views. We deal with irreconcilable differences on a case by case basis. We cope as best we can.

In Murphy Brown's case, after suffering through pregnancy and childbirth with her, we decided that if she wanted to become a single parent it was okay with us. We may not agree with her choice, but for her loyal viewers she is, after all, still part of the family. We will go along with her decision and hope for the best.

What the vice president hadn't quite grasped—along with many of the rest of us—is that values are not permanent and changeless. Rather, they are connected to a sliding scale of constantly changing social norms. The ''family unit'' is not what it once was, if indeed it ever was. It adapts to external influences, attitude changes, and the continual evolution of society.

Not so long ago, a program that featured an unmarried woman having a child would have been taboo on television. It simply would not have been aired. Censors would have considered it inappropriate and inconsistent with commonly held values.

Rewriting the Rules

Life was much simpler then. When World War II soldiers went off to fight on foreign shores, it was clearly understood by every red-blooded citizen that we were fighting to defend our very way of life. It wasn't the defense of an esoteric belief or a system of government. It was personal: the defense of a wife, 2.3 children, a cocker spaniel and a Cape Cod bungalow with a Chevy in the driveway.

Today, the lines aren't so clearly drawn. Women fight in combat, two-career families are ubiquitous, same-sex marriages are no longer novel, single parents are commonplace, and boomerang kids are returning home—sometimes with kids of their own.

---

[1]Ellen Goodman, ''Quayle's Poverty of Understanding,'' *Detroit News,* 26 May 1992, 11A.

Half a century after World War II ended, a third of the single men and one-fifth of the single women between twenty-four and thirty-five still live with their parents. Grandparents are moving in, and the segment of the population that is forming households at the most rapid rate is single adults over thirty-five.

If, before he lambasted "Murphy Brown," Vice President Quayle had walked over to the Department of Labor, he would have discovered that out-of-wedlock childbearing was the second most common source of new family formations. Nearly a quarter of the children born in recent years were to unmarried women.

Divorce, stigmatized by society only a few decades ago, has become so commonplace that we seldom give it a thought any longer. Extended families often include two sets of parents and multiple grandparents. Fully half of the couples married in the 1970s are expected to divorce.

Twenty-five percent of all children under eighteen live with one parent—nine of ten of them with their mothers—who have lower than average incomes.

Demographers, who study such things for a living, predict that these trends will continue well into the twenty-first century. The number of single parents will grow at a faster rate than the "traditional" married with children.[2]

Adjusting to the New Morality

Whatever your personal morality may be, you are simply going to have to adjust to working with, living next door to, being friendly with, and selling to customers who have wildly different values. The changes are already well under way to grant equal status and protect the rights of those with "alternative life-styles."

Not long ago, a New York court ruled that a gay couple could be considered a family under New York City's rent-control regulations, a decision that may have a major influence

---

[2]U.S. Bureau of the Census; James R. Wetzel, "American Families: 75 Years of Change," *Monthly Labor Review* (March 1990), 4–13.

in changing the legal and societal definition of a family. It may be the beginning of a new perception of exactly what constitutes a family in these uncertain times.

This single court decision has not yet rocked the foundation of the nuclear family, but already opposing sides are preparing for battles that are sure to follow. Gary Bauer, president of the Washington, D.C.–based Family Research Council and a former Reagan administration domestic affairs advisor, called the ruling a "dangerous landmark," one that many people find deeply disturbing and will not accept.[3]

Does it really matter on a personal level? If our friends, our neighbors, or our children choose a path that differs radically from our own, does that automatically make them wrong and us right? As civilization continues its relentless march into the future, those who will be happy and successful will be those who are tolerant of other points of view.

No Single Answers to Complex Problems

If there were a single right answer, we would surely have found it by now, and we could dispense with all other forms of government, religion, morality, and codes of ethics. There would be one rule book and we would all follow it. Of course, there has never been, is not now, and never will be one set of rules upon which we all agree. We are all very different in our genetic makeup and in the life experiences that have shaped us into the people we are.

Perhaps the stress and uncertainty we are experiencing are a function of our particular millisecond of history. We are living through the collapse of a way of life before its replacement has taken shape. Much like earthquake forces that build up from the gradual shifts of the plates of the earth's crust, the strain is likely to continue until a massive upheaval brings things back into alignment.

Those forces are already at work. American voters, unhappy with the state of government, are "throwing the rascals out"

---

[3]William Glaberson, "The New Family," *Ft. Lauderdale Sun Sentinel,* 16 July 1989, 1D.

in droves, annoyed in part with the failure of our representatives to deal with the tough questions and to rebuild the infrastructure to accommodate today's families.

Outdated Laws and Policies

Our laws are antiquated and our policies are outdated. Government's position on the family is based in large part on labor legislation—social security, unemployment and workers' compensation benefits—passed by Congress and signed into law by President Franklin D. Roosevelt during the 1930s. The New Deal period also spawned the National Labor Relations Act and the Fair Labor Standards Act, and in the 1940s, standard deductions and exemptions were added to national income tax law.

Laws enacted during that era "accepted and perpetuated the myth that every family had or should have had a Dad working, a Mom cooking and cleaning, and the kids doing their homework after school," according to *Dollars & Sense* magazine.[4] In reality, the laws probably never did address the needs of diverse families, and definitely slighted lower income people who have long needed two incomes to survive.

Certainly, things have changed considerably in the decades that have elapsed since the New Deal era. With both parents working in most families, there is no one to stay home with the kids—even when they are sick. We've seen a spate of news reports about "home alone" kids whose parents have left them to fend for themselves while adults do everything from going to work to taking a vacation.

With life expectancy continuing to lengthen, contemporary parents have also had to learn to deal with the problems of aging parents. The conflict between the children's and grandparents' needs has earned this group the label "the sandwich generation." They are caught in the middle, struggling to provide for family members at both ends of the generational spectrum.

---

[4]Patricia Horn, "Creating a Family Policy," *Dollars & Sense* (January/February 1990), 6.

Finding New Solutions

Employers have had to find new ways to help their employees cope with today's complex problems. Companies and unions are working together to develop child- and elder-care programs, developing referral networks, liberalizing leave policies, and allowing time off to handle family matters.

General Motors and the United Auto Workers Union have gone into the child-care business together. GM surveyed its 40,000 employees that work in thirteen plants and warehouses in the Flint, Michigan, area and found that they had 19,500 children under twelve years of age, 6,400 of whom were under six. GM and the United Auto Workers bought a 16,000-square-foot building, remodeled and refurbished it, converting it to the auto industry's first child-care and development center.

Located near Flint, the center opened in June 1992 to care for children who range from infants through twelve years of age. Kids are enrolled on a first-come, first-served basis, and prices are slightly below those of competitive child-care facilities in the area.

Institutionalizing "Grandmother's House"

In the opening ceremonies for the center, GM Vice President Richard O'Brien said he viewed the place as "grandmother's house" and recalled how his mother and father left their children in the care of grandparents when they were at work.

UAW Vice President Stephen P. Yokich told participants at the opening ceremonies that his mother left home every day at 5:00 A.M. for her job on a GM assembly line, and left him a list of things he was to do before and after school. "I always knew there was a better way," he said.[5]

Heightened interest in child care, brought about in part by changing family structures, suggests new ways of looking at

---

[5]Helen Fogel, "GM, UAW Set New Course for Kids' Care," *Detroit News*, 29 May 1992, 1E.

things and often requires innovative and sometimes complex programs to support them. Some employers are experimenting with flex time, shared positions, shorter work days, working at home, and other alternatives to the forty-hour week to allow workers to manage their schedules around family responsibilities.

The Family and Medical Leave Act, which President Clinton signed into law early in his administration, allows most workers to take up to twelve weeks of unpaid leave during any one-year period because of the birth or adoption of a child, the need to care for a seriously ill child, spouse, or parent or because of the worker's own serious illness. The law reflects the importance of child-care and family issues to a work force composed of single parent or dual career families.

Resisting Relocation

The changing family structure is affecting our willingness to accept blindly the company's decision to transfer us. During the glory days of International Business Machines, employees joked that IBM really was an acronym for "I've been moved," because of the company's propensity for relocating people to manage its explosive growth.

Janice Loyd, a sales executive with IBM, and her husband Mike were years ahead of their time in 1977 when they transferred to Atlanta from Indianapolis. Janice accepted a promotion to take over a new territory and Mike quit his job to stay home and raise their sons, Carl and Curt. As the "Mr. Mom" of his neighborhood, Mike was a frequent topic of conversation at the coffee klatches.

Mike went back to work when the kids got older, and today has his own construction business in Marietta, Georgia. IBM has downsized and struggled to maintain its technological edge in an increasingly competitive high-tech world. Janice accepted the company's buyout offer during one of its many consolidation moves. Sadly, in early 1993, Janice succumbed to a rare and particularly insidious form of cancer, leaving Mike suddenly alone and facing a new upheaval in his life.

By today's standards, the Loyds' parenting arrangements during the late 1970s would hardly raise an eyebrow, but it is becoming increasingly difficult to persuade employees to relocate. At one time, we would agree to move if the answer was positive to two of three questions: Is it good for my career? Is it good for the company? Is it good for my family? Nowadays, employees are more likely to expect affirmative answers to all three.

The move itself is difficult enough, but when it is complicated by trying to address the diverse needs of all members of the extended family and find a comparable position for the spouse who is moving to accommodate his or her mate, the odds are better in Las Vegas or Atlantic City.

Reluctant Companies

Companies are also less willing to foot the bill. With the average move costing tens of thousands of dollars while competitive pressures are simultaneously squeezing profit margins, alternatives are considered very carefully before deciding to relocate employees.

It has not yet become a massive problem, but executive search consultants report increasing difficulty in persuading people to accept positions that require them to relocate. For our own reasons in our own culture, we are becoming more and more like Europeans, who find little reason to leave friends, family, and the familiar surroundings of their birthplace.

Why on earth would a Parisian, for example, even consider leaving the culture and charm of the City of Lights to accept a position out in the provinces. Some things can't be measured in terms of money and position! We Americans, on the other hand, have always prided ourselves on our mobility and our willingness to tackle new frontiers. But, what do we do when the new frontiers are our decaying inner cities and our crumbling infrastructure? Our problems are the problems of a mature civilization and we are changing our attitudes to adjust to them. We seek permanence and stability.

An Island of Stability in a Sea of Change

The family unit has traditionally served this purpose. Although the definition of what constitutes a family may not yet be legally defined or universally accepted by society, it is still our island of stability in a sea of change.

As a topic of cocktail conversation the changing family structure may be interesting, but how does it affect us and our lives? My friend Jim Brown, a leading Canadian businessman and former chairman of one of the world's largest accounting and consulting firms, uses a tongue-in-cheek description of how most people react to change. He believes that, contrary to what they may be saying, they are thinking: "Let's look at the big picture. How does it affect *me*?"

Luckily, change usually occurs gradually over time, mercifully granting us time to adjust. By the time the family structure has changed radically, we will have had ample opportunity to adjust to new developments. The point is this: Those who adapt quickly and correctly anticipate change can profit from it.

Testing Our Value Systems

We are all going to have to realize that our value systems will be severely tested and our opinions shaken to their foundations. "Unusual" family configurations will produce people with "unusual" beliefs. We will have to accept as fact the view that there may be no correct answer or any number of correct answers. Patience and understanding will be the order of the day.

Older managers will have to find new ways to communicate with young workers whose experiences in no way resemble their own and who may be motivated by many things besides the traditional trappings of success—money, influence, and power. Young people who haven't a clue how older managers think will have to find common ground to pursue shared goals and objectives.

This may not be so different from generation gaps that have always existed, but the experiences are likely to be more prolonged and intense, the result of accelerated and more pronounced changes both in attitudes and demographics. Fewer people entering the work force as a result of declining birthrates will give workers more options and managers fewer. Authoritarian managers with little regard for their people may find themselves with no one to manage.

Succeeding in the New World Order

If your aspirations lie outside the corporate world, it's a safe bet that the successful entrepreneurs of the future will be those who offer products and services that meet the needs of people who are staying single, deferring childbirth, living longer—people who have neither the time nor the inclination to shop for what they want.

Not so long ago, finding a market for your products and services was relatively simple. One could pretty much figure out who might be a likely prospect based on age, income, job title, and location. Markets were segmented accordingly, advertising and promotional media were identified and scheduled, the sales force was trained, and the product was launched.

Legend has it that author and motivational superstar Zig Ziglar got his start selling pots and pans door-to-door. I'm not sure such salespeople even exist any more, but if they do, one hasn't come to my front door in years. Consumers today have endless choices of gourmet shops, boutiques, and catalogs that specialize in cooking paraphernalia along with an assortment of department stores that have a huge selection of cookware. That's pretty tough competition for door-to-door selling.

For years, encyclopedias were sold the same way. Commissioned salespeople could be pretty confident that just about every home held a viable prospect. They worked their way up and down the streets calling on mothers, urging them to help their kids become better students by purchasing their own set of reference books.

Today, mothers are pursuing careers of their own and encyclopedias are used as sales incentives in supermarkets. Publishing companies responded to changing attitudes and family structures with new approaches. Encyclopedias are sold by direct mail, in retail outlets, and are accessible by subscribing to a computer data base.

A contemporary Avon lady is more likely to be a corporate staffer than a housewife working to make a few extra dollars to supplement the family budget. When great numbers of women moved into the work force, Avon followed, tailoring its sales approach and product offerings to appeal to working women.

High-Tech Marketing

That's the kind of thinking we are going to have to employ as it gets increasingly tougher to segment markets and find new customers. As consumers increasingly turn to the home and family as a refuge from a crazy world and the mass media become too expensive to reach buyers effectively, we will have to find newer, more efficient ways to attract attention to our products and services.

It will become even more difficult as privacy legislation and other restrictions limit the amount of information about income, preferences, and buying habits that can be sold to credit card companies, magazines, direct marketing organizations, and others interested in selling something to the public. Developing a profile of potential buyers will become a complex, time-consuming, high-tech undertaking.

Buying will become a more interactive, relationship-based process in which the consumer calls the tune. Consumers will decide what, where, when, why, and how they will buy. Salespeople may never see their customers. The relationship will be strictly electronic with all communication taking place by telephone or computer. Successful salespeople will be those who can quickly identify what motivates their clients and customers and respond with products and services that meet their needs.

Learning from Politicians

As is often the case, help may come from serendipitous sources. If anything good ever comes from political campaigns, it may be that they tend to expand our knowledge about shaping messages to communicate to the masses. In the advertising community, Richard Nixon is credited with being the first presidential candidate to use television effectively to sway public opinion in his favor.

He learned from his disastrous debates with John Kennedy in 1960 that people form opinions based more on what they see on the tube, than on the issues. Young, dynamic, and charismatic, Kennedy appealed far more to voters than did the pallid, tired, cerebral Nixon. Kennedy was swept into office on a wave of public euphoria.

When Nixon ran again in 1968, he didn't make the same mistakes. He hired the experts to package slick TV commercials and hone his public image. He narrowly defeated Hubert Humphrey despite the advantages Humphrey enjoyed as the incumbent vice president.

In the campaign of 1992, Ross Perot further extended the boundaries. It was widely known that technology to reach people individually and in groups had existed for years with computers, cable television, satellite transmissions, telephones, computers, and videoconferencing. Futurists such as Buckminster Fuller have been kicking the idea around since the 1950s, saying for decades that technology was rapidly making our representative form of government obsolete.[6]

Why did we need a congressman or senator to vote on our behalf when it would be a simple matter to allow us to decide for ourselves. Pros and cons of key issues could be placed before the voters via television and we could express our views by calling a certain telephone number, responding by computer, or some other electronic vehicle. Perot was merely the first to take advantage of available technology, cleverly packaging his approach as an electronic town meeting.

The Global Family Unit

Our sense of family and community is being radically altered by the changes that are going on all around us. "Grandmother's house" may be a day-care center, and our extended family may include a support network of friends around the globe with whom we stay in touch by telephone. Buying relationships may be impersonal computer transactions or face-to-face meetings as we choose.

The anonymity and privacy that are available to us through such technology as telephone caller identification devices, fax machines, computers, and telephone answering machines allow us to choose how and when we wish to interact with others. Personal relationships are personal indeed, and our

---

[6]Prodigy interactive personal service; copyright 1992 Prodigy Services Company.

families—whatever their composition—are ours alone to nurture, develop, treasure, and enjoy.

Key Points and Action Items

1. Values and beliefs are not permanent and changeless. They evolve with changing social norms. We must adapt more rapidly than ever before.

2. Today, the family unit is no longer confined to a traditional model: husband, wife, and children. Success in the new environment will require tolerance, patience, and understanding of radically different lifestyles.

3. We are living through the collapse of one way of life without another to replace it. We will be required to reconcile conflicting values for a very long time before new values and belief systems become entrenched.

4. There are no correct answers and any number of correct answers. Flexibility is essential for success.

5. Companies, unions, and government will be required to work together to solve child- and eldercare problems in an age when everyone works to make ends meet.

4

A Firm Foundation

*No man is so foolish but he may sometimes
give another good counsel, and no man so
wise that he may not easily err if he takes
no other counsel than his own. He that is
taught only by himself has a fool for a master.*

—BEN JONSON

I grew up on a hardscrabble farm in Oklahoma among fiercely independent farm people who sprang from pioneer stock. For our ancestors, self-reliance was akin to survival; for us it was a matter of pride and heritage. I eventually concluded that the principal reason my relatives were so stubbornly independent was that they had no control whatever over most of the things that determined their fortunes. They were at the mercy of the elements, the bankers, and the government. Therefore, what they could control, they would control absolutely.

They also had a great deal of time to think, working alone in the fields. Keeping one's own counsel almost exclusively can lead to some pretty strong and closely held opinions. They didn't give advice much, and they didn't accept advice easily. No one could tell them what to do, when to do it, or how.

Such stubborn determination was as much a part of me as the color of my eyes. It was part of my genetic makeup.

I carried the burden of that independence well into adulthood. My attitude was that if someone wanted to help me, fine; if not, that was fine too. I could manage quite nicely on my own, thank you very much.

A Transformational Experience

On October 15, 1981, everything changed. I learned to ask for help, accept it, and be grateful for it. That day, our twin girls Amy and Betsy were born. They were two months premature, tiny, and very fragile. Merrilee, my wife, was exhausted after a grueling day and a half of labor. Her doctors had given her drugs to delay labor as long as possible in order to allow the infants to take advantage of the accelerated development that occurs when birth is imminent. The physicians hoped the additional time would allow their lungs to develop sufficiently so the newborns could survive.

Our situation was exacerbated by the fact that our community hospital did not have the neonatal intensive care facilities premature babies require. Our doctors searched desperately for a hospital that had the right equipment and the space available to accommodate them.

A Grim Prognosis

Seventeen hours after the first signs of labor, Merrilee was whisked into the delivery room at Prentice Women's Hospital in Chicago. She was physically and mentally exhausted, and I was a complete wreck. As we walked toward the delivery room, I asked the chief obstetrician about the prognosis. As compassionately as he could, he told me that at best the twins had a fifty percent chance of survival.

They did survive—perhaps some of that pioneer spirit that my ancestors passed on to me was in their genes, as well—but not without a struggle that began at birth and, for Amy, continued for years afterward. Betsy had her ups and downs, too, but after an experience when she stopped breathing for a few terror-inducing moments, she quickly shucked her life-support systems and began to develop normally.

Amy was born with hydrocephalus—water on the brain.

Actually, it's a condition in which the body overproduces or doesn't properly absorb the cerebrospinal fluid that cushions the brain and lubricates the spinal cord. Untreated, the fluid builds up and in infants separates the skull and enlarges the head, very quickly leading to seizures, blindness, coma, and death.

Using new medical techniques, neurosurgeons today can install an artificial, flexible tube inside the body that drains or "shunts" excess fluid. It's an ingenious contraption with holes like a drain tile in the end that is installed inside the head. The other end, which dumps into the abdominal cavity, is made like a Chinese lantern. When pressure builds up, fluid is absorbed through the "drain tile" end, and the "Chinese lantern" opens up. The fluid is then absorbed by the body.

That's the principle, anyway. It usually works pretty well, but when the shunt fails, it must be repaired or replaced surgically, and the surgery itself may further upset its delicate balance. The process is one of trial and error. Sometimes it works, sometimes it doesn't. In her eleven years of life, Amy has had twenty-four surgeries related to her hydrocephalus.

A shunt malfunction can occur without warning. When it does, it is accompanied by blinding headaches, seizures, and if not corrected within about forty-eight hours, the result could be permanent brain damage, a coma, or worse.

Getting into Action

When a problem occurs, immediate action is required. Merrilee phones the hospital and surgeons, makes arrangements for someone to care for Betsy, and finds me, wherever I am. We notify friends and relatives, cancel and rearrange appointments. Years of experience have helped us develop a support network that can respond instantly.

Merrilee has even learned to cut through red tape to have Amy admitted to the hospital without the usual time-consuming admitting procedures. After the problem is diagnosed, we do a hasty situation analysis and develop our plan. Merrilee usually devotes her full time and attention to Amy. I take care of house, the bills, and Betsy. We divide the phone calls to arrange for whatever help we need.

Living with Constant Stress

The stress caused by our inability to relieve Amy's incessant pain during those episodes, and the uncertainty that always accompanies her illness, is multiplied by dealing with the logistics and expense of lengthy hospital stays. In addition to the normal pressures of managing a home and career, we have been required to arrange for tutors or otherwise help Amy keep up with schoolwork at a time when it was very difficult for her to concentrate on anything besides her illness. It is unbelievably hard on her, but it also affects every other member of the family. Betsy so worried about her sister that when she was seven years of age, pediatricians feared she was developing ulcers.

During one particularly difficult round of problems, just hours before she was scheduled for surgery at New York University Hospital, Amy experienced a massive seizure. Surgeons frantically juggled other emergency cases to get her into the operating room immediately.

As they wheeled her away, Merrilee and I walked alongside the gurney attempting to reassure her. She no longer believed us when we told her this operation would be the one that would fix the pain; we had made the same promise too many times before. We could say nothing except that we loved her and hoped that it would work this time.

As Merrilee and I wearily returned to Amy's room to await the call that we could come to the recovery room when the surgery was over, Merrilee suddenly became dizzy. She collapsed soon afterward. A nurse helped me get her to the emergency room where she was treated for exhaustion and stress overload.

Amy's doctors learned of the situation when they came out of the operating room. They rushed to the emergency room— still in their surgical garb—to check on Merrilee and give us a report on the operation. As I watched two of America's most respected neurosurgeons kneel before Merrilee's wheelchair, obviously as concerned about her as about Amy, I realized how fortunate we were to have a support network composed of such kind and caring people.

A Call for Help

With Amy in the recovery room, Merrilee in the emergency room, and Betsy staying with the neighbors, I knew I had again reached the limit of my capacity. I could not manage alone. We tried not to take advantage of our friends and relatives, but my family, Merrilee's family, our friends, our neighbors, and at times total strangers helped us. I had long since learned to put aside my pride and ask for help when we needed it, and in so doing discovered that most people actually like to help. They don't want to intrude, so they wait to be asked.

I went to the pay phone around the corner from the emergency room entrance and called our friends Bob and Jean Nicholas in Atlanta. Hours before they had phoned to offer assistance, but I had turned them down, telling them that so far I was doing fine. I promised to call if I needed them. The time came much sooner than I had expected.

Jean threw a few clothes in a suitcase and caught the next flight to New York, arriving in the wee hours of the morning. She helped care for Amy, kept Merrilee company until she recovered, and lifted all our spirits.

Amy's doing great now. She's bright, happy, well adjusted, and doing fine in school. Her goal is to become a neurosurgeon or a neurologist. I have no doubt she will; she may even someday be the one who finds a cure for hydrocephalus.

A New Perspective

The rest of us are fine too, a little the worse for wear, but none permanently scarred by the experiences. It has helped us to put things into perspective. When Merrilee and I get annoyed with the girls for arguing, leaving their socks on the floor, or complaining about their homework, we pause for a moment to reflect and realize how lucky we are to have those kinds of problems.

Our situation is an extreme example that we wouldn't wish upon anyone, but it has been enlightening. When we felt sorry for ourselves, all we had to do was look around the hospital waiting rooms to see others who were far worse off than we were. In truth, we have been extremely fortunate. We have always had excellent health insurance, a relatively good income, and a stable family. Many others had far sicker kids, incredible financial problems, and little if any emotional support. One pediatric intensive care nurse told us that the hardest part of her job was watching patients' families go bankrupt—physically, financially, and emotionally.

Our experiences taught us that disaster can strike anyone at any time, whether or not they expect it or are prepared to deal with it. In fact, it often seems that the times when we are called upon to give the most of ourselves are those times when we have the least to give. Fortunately, we are all stronger than we think we are, and dealing with adversity only makes us stronger.

Crises Are Relative

We also learned that crises are relative. If it's happening to you, it is the most important thing in the world, whether it's related to your family, your job, or your health. At various times, existing conditions may require us to pay more attention to one aspect of our life than another, but in the end, things usually balance out. Problems occur when we become obsessed with a single aspect of our lives.

If we continually neglect our family and friends to focus exclusively on our careers or our business, the time will come when friends and family are no longer there for us. Of course, the reverse is also true. Too much socializing will have disastrous consequences on a career or business.

Life is a series of trade-offs. We sell our time for money, and we leave friends behind in order to accept a transfer that will benefit our careers. To function effectively in a complex society that is in constant flux, we require a stable support system, one that encompasses our coworkers, our families, our friends, and often extends to professionals who provide the medical, legal, accounting, and other specialized services we require.

Family Is Key Element of Support Network

The cornerstone of the support network is the family. The composition of the family may be changing, but it is the unit with which we interact most, the wellspring of our role models and our value systems. Indeed, some experts blame most of what is wrong in this country on the disintegration of the nuclear family.

Author William Tucker argues that we have created a culture that is at odds with nature. Instead of behaving as most other mammals do—females genetically programmed to bear and care for the young while males provide food for them— female human beings can conceive at any time of the year. With modern technology, they can decide when or *if* they wish to have children.

If things weren't difficult enough, Tucker says, our biology works against us. Male sexuality is inclined toward abandoning children and going on to having more, while women have a larger biological investment in the child.

Society has screwed things up even further. Ancient divorce laws were designed against biological inclinations of both men and women—and in favor of a family-oriented society. Fathers usually got custody of the children. The system made it difficult for men to "just dance off care-free. They had to take the children with them. On the other hand, if women wanted to divorce, they couldn't just 'take the children and run.'" Tucker believes that paternal custody discouraged divorce by making it much more painful for both parties.

He concludes his essay on the family with this warning: "Although the family has been with us since the beginning of human evolution, it remains a relatively fragile biological institution. The desires of individual men and women do not 'naturally' work in its favor. Without cultural reinforcement— or with wrong-headed social intervention—our biological drives can quickly carry us back to the earlier mother-and-her-children mammalian family."[1]

Maintaining a Family Unit Requires Work and Respect

Maintaining a caring, functional family unit requires work. It also requires respect for each individual member from the

---

[1]William Tucker, "Why We Have Families," *American Spectator* (December 1985), 14+.

youngest to the oldest, and from the minute they join the family. Whether a person becomes part of the family through remarriage, adoption, or is born into it, each must understand his or her role in the family and feel that he or she is an integral part of it.

Over the years, I've had the opportunity to work with privately held companies, huge Fortune 500 corporations, nonprofit organizations, and accounting, law, and architectural firm partnerships. It constantly amazes me how senior executives in a highly successful business can inspire and motivate thousands of employees, yet forget everything they know when they go home.

When I told one CEO's wife that he was one of the most patient and understanding people I had ever met, she said, "That's the problem. He uses it all up at work. When he comes home at night, he has nothing left for us."

With his family, he was a demanding, controlling person who managed his relationships with the most important people in his life more with threats and intimidation than with kindness and understanding. When his daughter decided to go to a university that he didn't approve of, he refused to pay the tuition. He "managed" his wife the same way. If she didn't behave as he thought she should, he cut her household allowance.

It surprised no one who knew them that their relationship eventually ended in a bitter divorce. He alternately tried to bribe or force the children to stay away from their mother, and ultimately destroyed his relationship with the entire family.

Happily, that's not the end of the story. He later remarried and began to work out his problems with his kids. I'm confident that they will come to terms, but at a very high—and unnecessary—emotional cost to everyone involved. Even if they couldn't live together, they could have parted company on a basis that was amicable enough to allow them to go on with their lives without attempting to destroy each other.

Importance of Friends

Friends are the next important link in your support network. Since most of us are influenced more than we like to admit by our friends, the type of people with whom we choose to associate is extremely important. Your mother was right: you will never bring them up to your level; they will only drag you down to theirs. Some experts have concluded that a group can never transcend itself. A few rare individuals may, but the group will always sink to the lowest common denominator. It is much easier to choose to associate with positive, happy, successful people than to transform negative failures into the kind of people you enjoy being around.

This is not to say that we should have nothing to do with people whom we dislike. To expect to do so would be totally unrealistic in our interdependent society. We work with unhappy, negative people, we do business with them, and sometimes we live with them. Positive people should make every effort to help others counter the negative influences in their lives.

I have enormous respect for people who devote their lives and careers to helping those less fortunate than themselves—ministers, priests, social workers, etc.—who are paid far too little for their contributions. Each of us needs to help share the burden, to help others whenever and wherever we can.

W. Clement Stone, whom many regard as the father of PMA—A Positive Mental Attitude—believes that when we help others without expecting anything in return, we set in motion a force for good that multiplies itself and comes back to us from many unknown sources. When we apply the Golden Rule in our dealings with others, they are encouraged to do likewise, as are the recipients of their good deeds. Goodwill expands geometrically.

We all need positive reinforcement. One of the first words a small child learns is "no." "No, you can't poke your finger in the electrical outlet. No, you may not dive off the balcony." It's a perfectly rational act on the part of parents. After all, teaching children what they *can't* do is the first step in preparing them for life's dangers. Unfortunately, all too often negative influences and emotions stay with us throughout our lives. We need positive input to cancel the negatives.

Help from Support Groups

Help is available. In addition to your cadre of positive friends, support groups have sprung up for just about every type of problem—real or imagined. If you have a physical or mental illness, overeat, drink or love too much—or have a friend or relative who does—there are others like you who meet weekly to benefit from sharing their experiences.

Support groups have supplanted organized religion or become the most popular programs a traditional church offers, and they are often more effective than family members in solving the problem, according to some experts. "After all," a *Newsweek* article on the topic says, "a dysfunctional family is often what brings people to support groups in the first place."[2]

With strangers, people can be brutally honest, and receive candid feedback in return. Since everyone else in the room has at one time been in a comparable position, they can't be fooled by lame excuses or empty promises. The focus is on accepting responsibility for one's own actions.

Much of the benefit may come from simply talking about the problem. Telling your story to others somehow lightens the load, even if the burden of solving the problem still rests squarely upon your shoulders. Participants find solace in sharing. Knowing that others have similar problems somehow makes it a little easier to bear your own, and by helping others, you help yourself.

According to the *Newsweek* account, support groups have even been successful in extending life. A ten-year Stanford University study revealed that terminally ill cancer patients who participated in support groups lived almost twice as long as those who only received medical care.

Support groups have become so popular in recent years that estimates place the number of meetings held weekly at around a half million, with some fifteen million people attending them. A National Self-Help Clearinghouse has been formed in New York, and most cities have a local equivalent designed to help you find the local chapter of a support group that interests you.

---

[2]Charles Leerhsen, Shawn D. Lewis, Stephen Pomper, Lynn Davenport, and Margaret Nelson, "Unite and Conquer," *Newsweek* (February 5, 1990), 50–55.

Paid Professionals

The final link of a strong support network is composed of paid professionals with expertise in specific areas. Most of us can't afford to hire experts to help us in every area we'd like; if we could, we would each have a physician, an attorney, an accountant, an investment banker, and perhaps a psychiatrist on our personal staff.

What we do have, however, are health insurance plans to fund medical and mental health care for our families, and books written by experts in other fields. We can learn the rudiments of investing, income taxes, and law so that we are sufficiently informed to ask the right questions. We are far more effective when we accept as fact that we can't do everything for ourselves and seek professional help from those who can best assist us. Intellectual arrogance can only lead to trouble.

Expert Advice Is Worth the Price

I've always considered myself a fairly intelligent person and I read and study to try to stay current with what's going on in the world. I've also watched "Perry Mason" and "L.A. Law" on television. Neither activity makes me a lawyer.

I learned this fact when I went to small claims court to try to collect for damages to my car resulting from a minor automobile accident. I had photos of the scene, measurements of the skid marks, and a model layout in which I could reenact the accident. It would have been great stuff for television, but it was no substitute for an understanding of law and courtroom procedures.

Time after time, the judge sustained my opponent's objection to my attempts to introduce my "evidence." The judge attempted to guide me, but I didn't even know enough about the rules of evidence to understand what he wanted me to do. Finally, in exasperation, I said, "I thought the purpose of small claims court was to simplify the procedures, to provide justice for the common man."

"It is," the judge responded. "That's why we have relaxed the rules of evidence." I lost the case without even mounting a good offense. I vowed that I would never again place myself in a similar position. If the situation called for a pro, I would engage one. Expert advice *is* worth what you pay for it.

Choosing Your Team

If you do decide you need professional help, what is the best method for choosing the right firm or person for the job? Most professional societies maintain lists of their members, but they will tell you little more than whether or not the person in question is a member in good standing. The American Medical Association, for example, won't tell you that your doctor has a long list of malpractice complaints lodged against him or her, nor will the American Society of Certified Public Accountants offer an opinion about the competence of its members.

Being a member in good standing means that the individual has completed the necessary educational requirements and passed appropriate examinations to be certified or licensed to practice in your state. However, this should be the first step in checking someone out, not the last. Professional organizations are reluctant to disbar, decertify, delicense, or in any way punish their members. They tend to give them the benefit of the doubt.

Check Them Out

Check service providers out with the Better Business Bureau. Your local BBB office will tell you whether or not clients have filed complaints about an individual, what type of complaints, and how many.

Ask for referrals. A decade and a half after restrictions on advertising by professional service firms were relaxed, most agree that the best source of new business is still a satisfied client. Ask your friends and neighbors who does their taxes or to which doctor they take their kids. You may not even have to ask. Most of us like to recommend those who do outstanding work, and we don't hesitate to complain to others if we are dissatisfied. In fact, market researchers who study such things tell us if a consumer is dissatisfied with a product or service, he or she will tell somewhere between ten and twenty friends, while they will tell only approximately one-third that number if they are happy with the product or service.

Trust Your Instincts

Finally—and most unscientifically—trust your instincts. If you don't have confidence in a person, don't retain him or her. You must often tell this person intimate details about your finances, your body, your failures—very private things—and if you are not comfortable with the individual, you may withhold critical information. You may hurt yourself by making it difficult for the professionals to do their best for you.

Ask questions. Don't be embarrassed if you don't know much about the subject. That's why you are hiring them. They are the experts; they've spent a lifetime learning the field. If they can't answer a question to your satisfaction in language you can understand, or if they patronize you, get away from them. They are not the kind of people you want in your support network.

Be skeptical. Professionals are supposed to be impartial, but everyone has opinions, preferences, and values. If they advise you to do something—and you've asked enough questions to make sure you fully understand their advice—that doesn't make sense to you in light of everything else you know, check it out. Get a second opinion from another professional in the field. Making a mistake in a serious matter will be far more expensive than paying for good advice.

Remember the old proverb: A chain is only as strong as its weakest link. So it is with your support network. You need strong family ties, good friends, and outstanding professionals whom you trust. They are your safety net. Knowing that your foundation is strong and secure gives you the confidence and courage you need to reach for your brass ring.

Key Points and Action Items

1. Few of us can succeed without help from anyone else. Learn to ask for help, accept it graciously, and give something in return.

2. The family is a fragile biological institution. Maintaining a strong family unit requires work and it requires respect for each individual member—from the youngest to the oldest.

3. Help is available to you from family, friends, support groups, and paid professionals. Know where and how to find the help you need.

4. Expert advice is worth what you pay for it. No advice or bad advice is far more expensive than not making the mistake in the first place.

5. Don't be afraid to question paid advisers. If they can't explain the solution in plain language that you can understand, the chances are good that they don't really know the answer themselves.

5

Evolution: From Carnegie to Today

Study the past if you would divine the future.

—CONFUCIUS

In 1908, a watershed event occurred in the history of modern motivation. It was then that a young writer named Napoleon Hill secured an interview with steel magnate Andrew Carnegie for the purpose of writing a profile about the great industrialist and philanthropist.

As Hill questioned Carnegie about the secret of his success, Carnegie lamented: "It's a shame that each new generation must find the way to success by trial and error when the principles are really clear-cut."[1]

According to Hill's account of the meeting, Carnegie challenged him to write about the principles, to learn the secrets of success practiced by the leaders of the day and to make them available to anyone who wished to apply them. At the time, Carnegie was in his early seventies, and had seven

---

[1] Samuel A. Cypert, *Believe and Achieve* (New York: Avon Books, 1991), xi.

years earlier sold his company (the corporate predecessor to U.S. Steel) to J.P. Morgan for over a half billion dollars, an immense fortune at the time. His plan was to give away his wealth to worthy causes, telling confidants, "I should consider it a disgrace to die a rich man."

Carnegie was a complex character. In his famous essay, "The Gospel of Wealth," he attempted to reconcile his devotion to "Social Darwinism" with Christian principles. He subscribed to the theory—popular with the nineteenth century elite—that in business as in nature, only the strongest survive. Although he generally rejected organized religion, his residual Christianity left over from his Presbyterian upbringing in his native Scotland convinced him that "the wealthy man was 'the mere trustee' of his wealth and therefore had a responsibility to use 'his superior wisdom, experience' and money to aid the poor."[2]

Carnegie and his family were skeptics. They distrusted the establishment both in Scotland and in America. Carnegie's father, a handloom weaver in Scotland, lost his job with the advent of steam-driven looms. He never fully recovered from the shock of unemployment, bankruptcy, and poverty that followed.

The Carnegie clan immigrated to America in 1849, held together by the strong will of Carnegie's mother until young Andrew was old enough to support the family. He idolized his mother and cared for her until she died. He did not marry until after her death; he was fifty-one years old at the time.

Driven to Succeed

He was driven by a desire to succeed at any cost, perhaps to avoid the humiliation his father experienced, perhaps to please his mother. In any event, he worked and studied tirelessly. According to Syracuse University history professor Vernon F. Snow, "Andrew Carnegie was wedded to his work and devoted to self-education throughout his early manhood.

---

[2]Joseph M. McShane, "The Centennial of Andrew Carnegie's 'Gospel of Wealth,'" *America* (October 7, 1989), 211–213.

"For him, America was the land of freedom and opportunity. He was ambitious, shrewd, and self-disciplined. He took advantage of opportunities; he also created opportunities for himself and others."[3] He was so obsessed with winning at any cost that decades after his death he is perceived by some as little more than a cruel tyrant who treated people badly until he was old, then gave away his money out of a sense of guilt and a warped desire to ensure that his heirs had to make their own way in the world.

Carnegie's early companies were either partnerships or associations formed with cash or collateralized credit; he disliked the corporate structure and the stock market upon which it was capitalized. His business was built upon the combined power of his associates, which he described as his "Master-Mind Alliance."

A Proponent of Continuous Learning

He attributed much of his success to the learning he pursued in his free time. He read voraciously on a broad spectrum of subjects and corresponded with many of the leading thinkers of his day. He synthesized his thoughts and publicized them in speeches, articles, and books.

Whatever his motivation, Carnegie so prized individual incentive and achievement that when he set out to give away his fortune, causes that topped his list were those aimed at helping those who had the desire to improve themselves: free libraries, public art galleries, parks, music halls, and technical schools. At the bottom of his list were churches (although he loved organ music and donated organs to thousands of churches) and swimming pools.

Throughout his life, he generated a good deal of controversy, a fact that apparently did not bother him in the least. He fought to end wars and promote world peace, and according to Professor Snow, relished the challenge of creating a new type of charitable organization in order give his money

---

[3]Vernon F. Snow, "Andrew Carnegie's Gospel of Wealth," *Society* (July/August 1991), 53–57.

away. The philanthropic organizational model that he invented has become the standard form for more than twenty-five thousand foundations today.

It is doubtful that Napoleon Hill loomed large in Carnegie's life. He is not mentioned in any of Carnegie's works, nor does his name appear in any of the many books written about Carnegie. Nevertheless, he was Hill's inspiration, and the impetus for the modern self-help movement. According to Hill's account, he assumed that when Carnegie challenged him to develop a philosophy of success that anyone could apply, the steel magnate was offering to underwrite the project.

A Writer's Challenge

He was stunned when Carnegie asked him if he was willing to devote twenty years of his life to researching the philosophy while supporting himself. " 'It is not my unwillingness to supply the money,' Carnegie said, 'it is my desire to know if you have in you the natural capacity for willingness to go the extra mile, that is, to render the service before trying to collect for it.' Successful people, Carnegie went on, are those who render more service than they are required to deliver."[4]

To get the project going, Carnegie provided introductions to wealthy and influential people of the early twentieth century, and paid some of Hill's travel expenses, but no more. He stuck to his terms; the young writer would have to support himself during his two decades of research and writing. Hill interviewed Henry Ford, Thomas Edison, John D. Rockefeller, Woodrow Wilson, William Howard Taft, James J. Hill, William Wrigley, Jr., and scores of others in his pursuit of the secrets of success.

Carnegie did not live to see the effect of the force he set in motion. He died in 1919, about eight years before Hill first published the philosophy he called the *Law of Success* in a series of eight booklets. True to the canny Scotsman's prediction, it had taken Hill almost twenty years to finish the work. Not surprisingly, the philosophy included the principle of Going the Extra Mile.

---

[4]Cypert, xi.

Napoleon Hill's Thirteen Principles

In 1937, Hill condensed his success philosophy in a little book he called—after much agonizing over what to title it—*Think and Grow Rich*. In it, he identified thirteen steps to riches.

The original thirteen principles included:

1. Desire: the starting point of all achievement.
2. Faith: visualization of, and belief in, attainment of desire.
3. Autosuggestion: the medium for influencing the subconscious mind.
4. Specialized knowledge: personal experiences or observations.
5. Imagination: the workshop of the mind.
6. Organized planning: the crystallization of desire into action.
7. Decision: the mastery of procrastination.
8. Persistence: the sustained effort necessary to induce faith.
9. Power of the Master-Mind: the driving force. (Based on Andrew Carnegie's concept, Hill defined the Master-Mind as two or more minds working in perfect harmony toward a common goal.)
10. The mystery of sex transmutation. (The general idea is to enjoy the sexual tension that exists between men and women without acting upon it, to use your sex appeal to reach your goals.)
11. The subconscious mind: the connecting link (to your conscious mind).
12. The brain: a broadcasting and receiving station for thought.
13. The sixth sense: the door to the temple of wisdom. (Instinct, intuition.)[5]

---

[5]Napoleon Hill, *Think and Grow Rich* (New York: Fawcett World Library, 1968), 1–6.

An Action-oriented Philosophy

The granddaddy of self-help books, not only did it tell the success stories of rich and powerful people, but for the first time a book revealed in an organized fashion the principles they practiced to achieve success. Hill told readers what to do to succeed and how to do it. The book became an immediate best-seller, and is the all-time best-seller in the motivational field. Millions upon millions of copies have been sold in several languages around the world.

Hill had much in common with Carnegie. He, too, was born into poverty and was greatly influenced by his stepmother. Napoleon Hill was born on October 26, 1883, in a one-room log cabin on the Pound River in the mountains of southwest Virginia. His father was barely able to feed and care for his family. His natural mother died when Hill was only eight years old.

With little parental guidance, young Hill quickly got into minor scrapes with the law and with others. He credits the turnaround in his life to his stepmother. She saw potential in Napoleon Hill that others did not, and she made it known very early in the marriage that she was not about to put up with living in poverty as the Hill family had been doing.

Years later, Hill recalled: "When I was a very young boy, I heard a dramatic speech on poverty by my stepmother a few days after she married my father and discovered the conditions we lived under in our mountain cabin in Wise County, Virginia. It made a lasting impression on me.

" 'This place we call a home,' she told my father, 'is a disgrace to all of us and a handicap to our children. If we stay here and accept this poverty, our children will grow up and accept it too.

Breaking the Poverty Cycle

" 'No matter how long it takes, or what sacrifices we have to make, I intend that our children shall have an education and better themselves. I don't know for the moment just when or how we'll make the break from this daily reminder of poverty, but I know we're going to make it.'

"And she did make it! Somehow she scraped up tuition to

send my father to Louisville Dental College so that he ultimately became one of the best-known dentists in southwest
Virginia.

"Then she moved up from our mountain home to the country seat of Wise into a tidy, comfortable house where her three
children and my father's two boys lived while they got an
education.

"She bought a typewriter and taught me to use it when I
was thirteen. Within a year she had me working as a 'mountain
reporter' for a dozen small newspapers.

"It was the inspirational guidance of this woman, refusing
to accept poverty, that helped influence me to accept Andrew
Carnegie's assignment to begin organizing the *Science of
Success*."[6]

Ahead of His Time

Hill was far ahead of his time in his understanding of left
and right brain functions, the subconscious, nutrition, and
many other aspects of human behavior. Most of the principles
he defined were pragmatic, sensible, and applicable to daily
life. He identified a process that any one of us could use to
reach any goal we set for ourselves.

Because in his writings he occasionally wandered into topics bordering on mysticism, his works were sometimes derided
by skeptics, but his readers gave him the benefit of the doubt.
If he wanted to dabble in things they did not fully understand,
it was okay with them. Perhaps he knew something they
didn't. He authored several best-selling books based on the
philosophy he spent a lifetime refining, lecturing, and writing
about.

W. Clement Stone's Discovery

One who found reinforcement for his own philosophy in
Hill's practical approach to motivation was W. Clement Stone.
Born on Chicago's tough South Side in 1902, Stone began
working at the age of six, hawking newspapers on the street

---

[6]Napoleon Hill, "Anyone Can Overcome Poverty," *Success Unlimited* (January 1963), 27.

corner. He soon learned about competition as the older news-boys muscled their way into the busiest corners, relegating younger, smaller boys like young Stone to less desirable locations where traffic was lighter and sales fewer.

The plucky lad didn't give up; he simply changed his strategy. He went into Hoelle's, a popular restaurant in the area, and began selling papers to patrons. The owner quickly tossed the boy out, but he kept returning. After several replays of the incident, Mr. Hoelle threw up his hands and said, "What's the use?" He and Stone eventually became great friends and he allowed the young salesman to work in the restaurant without interference.

The lessons Stone learned as a newsboy stayed with him throughout his life. He learned to go where prospects were concentrated in the greatest numbers, to size up prospects quickly, to maximize his efficiency by not wasting time futilely trying to persuade those who would not buy, and never to give up until he had reached his goal.

Those were exactly the principles he used to build Combined Insurance (since merged with Ryan Insurance to become the giant Aon Corporation), a company he founded in 1922 with $100 and a Positive Mental Attitude, into a multinational insurance empire. He went into office buildings and factories and sold insurance policies to the people that worked in them. As the business grew, he hired other commission salesmen.

In 1937, Morris Pinckus, a well-known sales trainer at the time, gave Stone a copy of a new book that he was selling to sales managers to help them motivate their sales forces. The book, written by a relatively unknown writer named Napoleon Hill, was titled *Think and Grow Rich*. The philosophy that Hill espoused so coincided with Stone's own beliefs that he, too, began the habit of helping others by giving them self-help books.

Motivational Jackpot

Recalling the incident fifty years later, Stone said, "I mailed a copy of *Think and Grow Rich* to my salesmen, and Bingo! I hit the jackpot. Big things began to happen for me. My sales managers began to build super salesmen, and my salesmen began to achieve such phenomenal results that they seemed unbelievable to those who had not learned the art of motivation.''

In his best-selling book, *The Success System That Never Fails*, Stone wrote this tribute to the little book with the big ideas: ''Within two years after I received *Think and Grow Rich*, I again had over a thousand licensed representatives.'' (He'd lost most of his sales force and struggled to stay in business during the depression.) ''My bills were paid, I had a savings account and other equities, including a winter home— a modern duplex at Surfside, Florida.

''Although there is no real way to prove it, I believe that *Think and Grow Rich* has inspired more persons to business and financial success than any book written by a living author.''[7]

Despite their shared philosophy and interests, Stone and Hill didn't meet until fifteen years later. Until they shared the dais at a Chicago North Shore Kiwanis Club meeting, Stone did not realize Hill was still living. Hill was very much alive, but at sixty-nine was semiretired, enjoying the fruits of a lifetime of writing and lecturing. Stone, at fifty, was chairman of Combined Insurance Company.

The program chairman, who had arranged for the speakers to meet (each was unaware of the other's attendance until they were seated), hoped the two would enjoy each other's company. They emphatically did. Before the luncheon was over, Stone had persuaded Hill to come out of retirement and collaborate on a series of books, tapes, seminars, and self-help courses. Hill had one condition to the deal: Stone would serve as his general manager.

A Powerful Partnership

For ten years, the two circled the globe, telling the story of success through positive thinking. They published several books and lectured about their philosophy to thousands of people. ''Club Success Unlimited'' based on the principles they taught sprang up all over the country.

---

[7]W. Clement Stone, *The Success System That Never Fails* (New York: Pocket Books, 1980; published by arrangement with Prentice-Hall, Inc.), 161–162.

To give followers a regular infusion of positive thinking, they founded *Success Unlimited*, a magazine for achievers. It was the forerunner of today's popular *Success!* magazine. Their book, *Success Through a Positive Mental Attitude*, was translated into several languages and is today hailed as a classic in the field of motivational literature.

Over the course of the decade they worked together, they continued to refine the philosophy, eventually expanding Hill's original thirteen steps to riches into what they considered to be seventeen essential principles of success. The seventeen were:

1. A Positive Mental Attitude.

2. Definiteness of Purpose.

3. Going the Extra Mile.

4. Learning from Defeat.

5. The Master-Mind Alliance.

6. Teamwork.

7. Applied Faith (Your faith in God, in yourself, and in your fellow man—in action).

8. Cosmic Habit Force/Universal Law (All things in nature behave in predictable patterns or habits. You can form good habits or bad ones as you choose—by repetition.)

9. Personal Initiative.

10. Enthusiasm.

11. A Pleasing Personality.

12. Self-Discipline.

13. Budgeting Time and Money.

14. Maintaining Sound Physical and Mental Health.

15. Creative Vision (imagination, using the subconscious).

16. Controlled Attention.

17. Accurate Thinking.

Perpetuating the Philosophy

To ensure the perpetuation of a philosophy that helped millions begin to understand and tap their hidden inner potential, the two turned their attention to The Napoleon Hill Foundation, now based in the Chicago suburb of Northbrook, Illinois. At his own expense, Stone bought the rights to all of Hill's books, manuscripts, and recordings, and donated them to the foundation. Those works are the underpinnings of the many outreach programs the foundation sponsors, and also provide a wealth of material for new publications.

His work completed, Hill retired once again in 1962. He lived in North Carolina until his death in 1970 at the age of eighty-eight. Stone, at ninety, lives in a villa overlooking Lake Michigan in north suburban Chicago. He continues to serve as chairman of The Napoleon Hill Foundation as well as in leadership positions of many other civic and philanthropic organizations. Like Andrew Carnegie, he has given away much of his wealth to worthy causes.

Most of today's success philosophies spring from the Andrew Carnegie, Napoleon Hill, W. Clement Stone connection. Many found mentors and supporters in Hill and Stone. Og Mandino had lost his home, his job, his family, his dream of becoming a writer, and with his last thirty dollars bought a gun with which to commit suicide when he found in a library in New Hampshire a copy of *Success Through a Positive Mental Attitude.*

He applied for a job with Combined Insurance, and in applying the philosophy he had learned from self-help books, discovered the truth for himself: "You really can accomplish anything you want, providing you are willing to pay the price."

His successes multiplied and the home office in Chicago began to notice him. He rented a typewriter, took two weeks off, and wrote a sales manual, "hoping someone in the company would recognize the great writing talent they had out in Maine."

Mike Ritt, now executive director of The Napoleon Hill Foundation, did notice. He offered Mandino a job as a writer.

From that humble beginning, Mandino became editor of *Success Unlimited* magazine, and went on to write several bestselling books. He is a popular speaker and lecturer, and has appeared on hundreds of radio and television programs. In 1983, he was the recipient of the first Gold Medal Award for literary achievement given by The Napoleon Hill Foundation.

Others whose names are synonymous with modern motivation were influenced by Hill and Stone. In the early 1980s, I covered for Stone's publishing arm the last "success rally" sponsored by *Success!* magazine and the Stone organization. In addition to Stone himself, on the dais that day were: Dr. Robert Schuler, Zig Ziglar, Denis Waitley, Mary Kay Ash, Paul Harvey, and the mayor of Chicago.

A New Collaboration

In the early 1980s, I worked as a free-lance editor of Stone's *PMA Advisor*, a newsletter published for business managers, sales executives, and entrepreneurs, and wrote an occasional article for *Success!* magazine. In 1985, I approached him with the idea of revisiting the seventeen principles of success to see if they still held up in contemporary society. It had been twenty-five years since he and Hill had written about the philosophy, and a great deal had changed since then.

The result was *Believe and Achieve*, a book that updated the philosophy and grouped the principles according to categories: Intellectual Principles, Personal Principles, Attitudinal Principles, Fraternal Principles, and Spiritual Principles. Simply stated, to be successful, you must use your brain, you need some personality, the right attitude, the ability to work with others, and you must believe in something larger than yourself. Each of these categories will be covered in detail in succeeding chapters of this book.

In *Believe and Achieve*, we also covered a couple of points Stone felt had not been fully explored in previous works. Although the ideas are closely linked, they are separate and distinct.

New Techniques

The first is what Stone called the R2A2 principle—Recognize and Relate, Assimilate and Apply information from any field that will help you reach your goal. When you have an established goal that you have a burning desire to achieve, you will find help from totally unexpected sources. Be alert for any information or idea that can assist you.

The second point Stone emphasized was the importance of creative thinking time. His advice is to set aside at least a half hour each day to do nothing but study and think. Choose the time of day that is best for you, when you can relax and totally focus on the subject at hand. Allow ideas to incubate and develop in your subconscious. You will be amazed at the results.

Thousands of scholars, psychologists, pop psychologists, authors, teachers, ministers, executives, and others have attempted to understand what inspires us. Motivational books, tapes, videos, and seminars have become a cottage industry. There are any number of approaches, and yet, not a great deal is known about the specifics of *what* motivates people to succeed.

What Motivates Us?

Some think we are driven by a Protestant work ethic that encourages individual responsibility. Others believe it is our love of competition that spurs us. Still others say it is peer pressure or status consciousness that propels us to high levels of achievement. Many say it is money. The accumulation of wealth is the only real measure of success, they believe.

As American society puts the excesses of the 1980s behind us, however, we seem to be less preoccupied with acquiring money for its own sake. We've learned that all things come with a price tag attached. Perhaps we are finally beginning to realize that true success is a balance between independence, self-satisfaction, pride in achievement, money, self-esteem, friendship, and spirituality—all with an eye toward leaving the planet in a reasonable condition for our children and grandchildren.

The Importance of Balance

Carnegie, Hill, and Stone understood the importance of balance. Carnegie viewed himself as a steward of wealth that should be returned to the public, sold his business when in his sixties, and spent the remainder of his life developing what he believed was a fair system of allocating funding to help people help themselves.

Hill wrote about the importance of maintaining a balance between time for work, sleep, and leisure. Most of his books also included recommendations for a balanced, healthy diet, and suggestions for maintaining sound physical and mental health.

Stone's anchor was his personal "magnificent obsession": to make this a better world for this and future generations. He has spent the past several decades helping others learn his philosophy of success through positive thinking, and he has given away millions to help fund worthwhile endeavors in this pursuit.

Both Hill and Stone strongly believed in the power of the Golden Rule. When you do something for someone else with no expectation of anything in return, Stone has often said, you set in motion a force or power that will return an infinite number of good things to you, often from completely unexpected sources. One good deed begets another.

Perhaps the most eloquent expression of the proverb that "what goes around comes around" came in 1932 from an Oglala Sioux holy man named Black Elk. He said:

"The Power of the World always works in circles, and everything tries to be round ... The sky is round, and I have heard that the earth is round like a ball, and so are all the stars. The wind, in its greatest power, whirls. Birds make their nests in circles, for theirs is the same religion as ours. The sun comes forth and goes down again in a circle. The moon does the same, and both are round. Even the seasons form a great circle in their changing, and always come back again to where they were. The life of a man is a circle from childhood to childhood, and so it is in everything where power moves."[8]

Perhaps we have come full circle.

---

[8]John G. Neihardt, *Black Elk Speaks* (New York: Pocket Books, 1932), 164–165.

Key Points and Action Items

1. The principles of success are clear-cut, and they can be learned and applied by anyone. Take the time to learn them and expend the effort required to implement them.

2. An effective motivational philosophy is not static. It evolves with the times and has a bias for action. Learn from those who have gone before, and adapt their thoughts to meet your needs.

3. Adopt W. Clement Stone's R2A2 principle. Recognize, relate, assimilate, and apply the knowledge you gain in any field to help you reach your goals.

4. Allow time for study and creative thinking. Set aside at least one half hour each day when you can relax and totally focus on the subject at hand.

5. Strive for balance in your life. Allow time for work, sleep, and leisure. Follow a balanced diet and maintain a positive attitude to ensure that you are physically and mentally healthy.

6

Transforming the Paper Society

Business is like riding a bicycle. Either you keep moving or you fall down.

— JOHN DAVID WRIGHT

When large companies began experimenting with electronic mail a few years ago, the initial euphoria that accompanied the ability to send messages by computer to any other person on the network was dimmed by the discovery that this new technology attacked the very foundations of a typical pyramidal organizational structure. Ordinary workers could avoid the chain of command and—horror of horrors—send a message directly to the CEO.

Such subversion was quickly arrested. Secretaries were assigned the task of reading the boss's E-mail and printing out messages deemed worthy of the chief's attention. Others were trashed or routed to others to handle. Once again, bureaucracy had triumphed.

The bureaucracy's success in suffocating this innovation was, of course, temporary. Organizations learned to deal with new methods of communication, and the more visionary executives quickly learned to appreciate the convenience and productivity improvement made possible by the application of new technologies. Busy people could transmit messages to other busy people; they could leave voice mail messages and they could send faxes from their automobiles. Equally busy recipients could respond at their convenience.

Distrusting Computers

Naturally, not everyone in every organization is wildly enthusiastic about the inevitable move toward such electronic linkups. Many of the children of the thirties, forties and early fifties—who are today's bosses—don't trust computers and don't know how to use them.

They place great value on the written word; the fact that the words were often generated by a computer is incidental to them. They read books, magazines, and newspapers, and they write letters, memos, and reports. Influencing them requires understanding how they think and relating to them in methods and language they understand.

"Sixty Minutes" sage Andy Rooney once aired a commentary about his lack of skill with a computer. He has one on his desk, but when he writes, he uses his old, trusty Underwood typewriter. He is obviously not alone in his inherent dislike of the "newfangled" machines.

At issue in the business world, of course, is not the technology itself, but our fear of its influence upon us and the changes it brings in our lives. Among the many changes the technological revolution has wrought is the ability to flatten traditional hierarchical structures.

Reinventing the Corporation

PepsiCo CEO Wayne Calloway, like other forward thinking executives, says that in today's complex business structures, we need to reject the old style of management and reinvent the corporation—from the bottom up.

"It seems to me," Calloway told PepsiCo's accounting firm partners, "for the past seven decades virtually every industry in the United States has been run on a single management structure. It was rigid, authoritarian, and based on a fundamentally pessimistic view of human nature. It was rooted in the traditional military hierarchy with layer upon layer of authority. The ruling motto was: 'you can expect what you can inspect.' The theme was control, control, control.

"Perhaps the most high-profile proponent of this management style in modern times was not an industrialist, but the legendary FBI chief J. Edgar Hoover. Hoover ruled his agency with an iron fist. He signed off on every decision, set parameters for every action, and struck fear into every employee.

"Hoover even laid down strict rules for agency memos, specifying exactly how many inches should be left for side margins. One day he received a memo with the margins too small. In big red letters, he scrawled an angry warning across the top: *Watch the borders!* The next morning, his frightened assistants transferred 200 FBI agents to Canada and Mexico."[1]

Calloway believes that's the organization of the past, when employees were more concerned about security and certainty. Today's employees value freedom and independence to operate without someone looking over their shoulders.

Teaching Eagles to Fly in Formation

The PepsiCo chief practices what he preaches. The company recruits motivated people, trains them well, empowers them, and turns them loose. "We take eagles and teach them to fly in formation," Calloway says. Managers are encouraged to take calculated risks, constantly to try new ideas, to attack the status quo. "The worst maxim around is 'Don't fix it if it ain't broke,'" Calloway told *Fortune* magazine. "You'd better be improving it because your competitor is. In this freewheeling culture," *Fortune* says, "a committee is defined as a dark alley down which ideas are led to be strangled."[2]

The company sets high goals for all its people, and rewards their success by elevating expectations for the next year. In this fast-track environment, good people are promoted quickly, and poor performers are weeded out. With the help of a strin-

---

[1]Remarks to KPMG Peat Marwick annual partners meeting in Orlando, Florida, October 5, 1990.
[2]Brian Dumaine, "Those Highflying PepsiCo Managers," *Fortune* (April 10, 1989), 79.

gent performance evaluation system, at the end of every year, each of the company's twenty thousand managers knows exactly where he or she stands.

They are also paid well and afforded the perks that go with a first-class organization. PepsiCo's philosophy is that it is cheaper to reward people for outstanding performance than to create a big bureaucracy to follow people around in an attempt to keep down costs.

PepsiCo: Leading the Way

PepsiCo is one company that is leading the move away from the paper society, using the power of technology to flatten hierarchies, empower people, and change the way it does business. PepsiCo has a formal program it calls SharePower to push power, money, and people out into the field—closer to the consumer. An accountant by training, the fifty-six-year-old Calloway calls the age of information "our age. We frolic in the sea of numbers and data and statistics," he says.

"Under the old, rigid hierarchies, a peculiar phenomenon occurred. At the top of any industrial organization, you had a handful of people with the power to make decisions. But these men and women sat in their offices in headquarters and received sales reports—sometimes two months after the fact. The information was not only late, but often filtered between four levels of bureaucracy.

"Meanwhile, out on the front line at the bottom of the pyramid, you had people with little power who were blessed with the richest and rawest treasure trove of information. So the higher you rose in the organization, the more power you earned, and the less information you had, until—finally—you got to be CEO. You could do anything you wanted without knowing what was going on!

"I exaggerate," Calloway says, "but I think you understand the problem. I think you also know the answer: the computer. Computers compress time. They can shrink oceans, and they can eliminate the gap of knowledge between the salesman on the front lines and the CEO in back."

Frito-Lay's Approach

The PepsiCo chief uses Frito-Lay as a good example of how the company used technology to eliminate paperwork and improve productivity while simultaneously improving the amount and quality of information reported up the line. "Here's how things worked in the 'old days'—meaning the mid-1980s. Our ten thousand Frito-Lay route salesmen spent an hour or two at the end of every day filling out pages of paperwork detailing their sales of Fritos, Doritos, and other products.

"Maybe a week later, a lengthy printout of this information was available at the regional office. By the time it all got back to headquarters, was consolidated, analyzed, and interpreted, it could be a couple of months. Only then would we have a rough idea of what was really going on in the marketplace.

"The hand-held computer has changed all that. Now the chairman of PepsiCo Worldwide Foods can sit in his office and figure out exactly how Doritos did last week in Aisle Four of the local Piggly Wiggly's . . . The hand-held computer is an amazing tool of analysis. It's productive. We estimate we save our salesmen at least five hours of paperwork a week. In fact, we've been able to add four hundred sales routes without hiring an extra driver, and now we have information not six weeks later like we used to, but one week later and sometimes even quicker."

Management Temptation

The problem Calloway sees with the massive amounts of data today's managers have available is the temptation for executives to attempt to fix the problems themselves, demotivating employees and killing the empowerment movement. "As those great numbers flash across our computer screens every morning," Calloway believes, "the J. Edgar Hoover that beats beneath the breast of every upper-level executive might reawaken. As the British magazine *The Economist* said, 'If you think computers can change human nature, you are either a management consultant, a liar, or both.'

"Let's imagine what would happen if Michael Jordon (the

former CEO of PepsiCo Worldwide Foods who has since left to join a private investment firm) looks at his computer one morning. He sees the sales of Doritos plummeting in the local Piggly Wiggly. He calls the salesman himself to tell him how to fix it.

"The salesman probably responds like this: first his secretary tells him Mike Jordon is on the phone. His immediate reaction is to think, 'What the heck is an NBA All-Star doing calling me?' Then he looks at the Frito-Lay organizational chart. He realizes, oh no, it's the Big Kahuna himself. My boss's, boss's, boss's, boss. After talking to Mike, he probably thinks, 'If that guy's worried about Doritos sales in aisle four, then I sure don't need to worry about them. I'll just wait to hear from him again. It's his responsibility, not mine.'

Potential of Information

"While the threat to organizations is very real, the potential benefit is even greater. If we use the new information with vision and discipline, it can be the tool to reinvent the corporation, to free both the old leader at the top and the new leader at the bottom. The challenge today's leaders have is to resist the urge to go back to the old days and try to control all the microdecisions—like fixing sales in aisle four of the local Piggly Wiggly.

"It's not easy. But if we can do it, we end up with much stronger leaders. Meanwhile out on the front lines, in the stores and restaurants, men and women will have the freedom and authority to not only see what's going on, but to act upon it. We end up with much stronger enterprises.

"We must use information in the context of our employees and their new value systems. Make it a tool of freedom, instead of an instrument of control. Because, in so doing we can give our nation more competitive companies, more fulfilled workers, and goods and services of a quality never thought possible," Calloway says.[3]

---

[3]Wayne Calloway, KPMG Peat Marwick remarks.

A Paper Explosion in the Paperless Society

Ironically, the very high-tech gadgetry that was expected to lead us toward the paperless society has triggered a paper explosion. Consumption of writing and printing paper in the U.S. went from less than seven million tons in 1959 to over twenty-four million tons four decades later—a 250 percent increase. The volume of mail continues to grow equally rapidly. Estimates place the 1992 volume at well over 160 billion pieces.

Says *Forbes* magazine: "The paperless office, the bookless library, the printless newspaper, the cashless, checkless society—all have gone the way of the Empire State Building's dirigible mooring, the backyard helipad, the nuclear-powered convertible, and the vitamin-pill dinner."[4] The technology comet that was expected to herald an electronic age has brought with it a long trail of supporting documentation in the form of credit card copies, bank statements, envelopes, checks, receipts, and the like.

We are, however, making progress. We are gradually overcoming our fears that unless we have a piece of paper to verify a transaction, our funds will be gobbled up by a hungry computer glitch. More and more of us are allowing our paychecks to be deposited in our bank accounts electronically. But most of us still get a paper copy—that looks like a paycheck—to assure us that the deposit was actually made.

Cash machines and gas pumps that accept credit cards and bank debit cards now ask us if we want a paper receipt or not. I suspect most of us still feel more comfortable if we have a paper record that we can produce when the bank statement alleges that we bought a thousand dollars worth of gas—instead of the ten bucks' worth we actually purchased. Too many humans who made errors and blamed them on their computers have made us leery.

---

[4]"The Computer Has Triggered a Paper Explosion," *Forbes* (May 29, 1989), 19–20.

Technology Drives Flatter Organizations

Nevertheless, the flatter organizations that PepsiCo's Calloway describes require computers to make them work. Executives will need vast amounts of data synthesized into usable information to understand what's going on in their far-flung empires. Overcoming their resistance will require computers to become even easier to use than they are today, something that is not far away.

We are not far from Apple CEO John Sculley's "transparent technology" that makes the computer so easy to use that we scarcely realize we're using one. Many contemporary user-friendly models can tell us the basics of how to use the machine and how to run the software, and the most advanced models offer user "manuals" on compact discs.

Today's hottest technology companies are those involved in networking. With the need to transmit information swiftly around the globe, companies want to be able to link various technologies into a single system. Xerox Corporation has responded with what it calls a document processing system that includes a desktop computer, printer, network, and scanner. The idea is to be able to store information that can be accessed by workers around the world, revised, edited, and moved back and forth between their computers at will.[5] Other companies offer similar options; some also include options that allow the operator to send faxes directly from a computer to a fax machine without ever printing a paper copy.

Improving Efficiency

Technological advances have greatly improved our ability to gather, organize, and process information. I wrote my first book on a portable typewriter. My secretary retyped my rough draft and she and I edited and proofread the manuscript end-

---

[5]Brian Dumaine, "What the Leaders of Tomorrow See," *Fortune* (July 3, 1989), 55.

lessly. By the time I had sufficiently recovered from the first book to attempt the next, I had acquired a cumbersome, bulky, magnetic card typewriter. By today's standards, it was terribly inefficient, but at the time it was a huge improvement over what I had been doing.

The book consumed two boxes of magnetic cards and although the system did allow one to move text and make corrections, it was very primitive. Mistakes were difficult to catch and revisions were tedious and time-consuming. When personal computers came along, the productivity improvements they allowed were astounding. Text could be moved around, edited, deleted, or otherwise manipulated with ease. Scissors and tape were replaced by computer icons, and the tools of the writing trade—dictionaries, thesauruses, and even grammar-checking databases—were contained in computer software programs.

No longer is it necessary to retype and endlessly revise and reprint paper manuscripts. My last book was written, edited, and revised on the computer screen. The computer disk which contained the entire text of the book accompanied the written manuscript when it was shipped to the publisher. The disk was converted to galleys by the typesetter, an enormous savings of time, money, and brainpower for all involved. I've learned to type as well and as fast as my secretary, and she is now free to do more challenging and more productive tasks.

High-Tech Library

Secondary research has been equally advanced. Instead of poring over books at the library, my writing partner, my wife, Merrilee, scans a microfiche reader or a computer terminal, or calls up one of the many data bases to which we subscribe on our home computer. A search program on the computer allows it quickly to find key words and topics, radically reducing the amount of time it takes to find needed information.

Soon, we won't even have to transcribe interviews; several computer companies already have the basic technology to convert—and even translate from other languages—spoken words into their written counterpart. Contemporary journalists write on computer terminals that are networked with other writers and editors, and with graphic artists. Instead of being sent to the composing room for typeset and layout, the finished work is converted electronically to type.

Finished layouts—including color graphics and photography—are digitized and transmitted via satellite to printing plants all over the world. On the receiving end, pages can be modified to include local information and regionalized advertising. Late-breaking news can be quickly incorporated into your *Wall Street Journal* or *USA Today*, printed in the wee hours of the morning, and delivered to your doorstep for you to peruse with your morning coffee.

Personalizing Communication with Advanced Technology

Sophisticated direct marketing companies such as Lands' End and L.L. Bean can accumulate data about your buying habits that allow them to tailor catalogs to your interests. If you are a fisherman and your neighbor is a golfer, your catalog may have a section on fishing rods while Gordon across the street may receive information about high-tech golf clubs.

A decade ago, in a handbook for business communicators, I wrote:

"In business communication today, advances in technology are being made so rapidly that it is difficult for the most practiced observer to fully understand the capability we have. Extensive data bases can be accessed by computer terminals that are not much larger than a conventional typewriter. Literally at your fingertips is complete information companies furnish to their shareholders and everything that has been published about a particular topic.

"There is no doubt that considerably more information is available today—about almost any topic we can imagine—than we can assimilate. Technology has enabled us to dish out far more than we can take in. As a result, it is more important than ever to distill the message whenever possible and to arrange it in a fashion that can easily be scanned by the reader to determine which of the materials is most pertinent.

A Visual Society

"The fact that we are a visually oriented society underscores the need for clear writing and can be used to your advantage. Every adman worth his fifteen percent knows that in print ads or direct mail it is a good idea to use more graphics and less copy if the audience is under forty. The generation that learned the alphabet by watching 'Sesame Street' responds to good graphics.''[6]

Technology has advanced more than I imagined in the ten years that have elapsed since I wrote those words. The now fifty-year-olds to whom I referred can use their executive information systems to distill reams of data into concise, actionable information, and they can review it in simple charts and graphs at their option. They may still be avid readers, but odds are that the day is not far away when much of their reading will take place on a laptop computer.

The transformation is already well under way, despite the entrenched resistance of the paper generation, as society begins to realize that computers can help us do things better, faster, and in more innovative ways. We are very quickly reaching the point where intellectual property may be worth considerably more than bricks and mortar.

Danger: Painful Change Ahead

This does not mean that the change will be painless. It won't be. The pain is intensified because we are trying to force new technology into an old organizational model, according to *PC/Computing* magazine. Simply adding new technology isn't enough. We have to change the way we do things. We have to empower our employees to think on their own and to move quickly. The computer gives us the capability; the organization must give us the power.

The companies that prosper in the age of technology will be those that have a shared vision and act upon it. Intelligent employees who understand the company's mission and where they fit into it will make sound decisions and contribute to the company's overall success.

Leaders of tomorrow will be those who find better ways to

---

[6]Samuel A. Cypert, *Writing Effective Business Letters, Memos, Proposals, & Reports* (Chicago: Contemporary Books, 1983), 3, 75.

get critical information from the front lines to the executive suite and can figure out how to extract important information from the huge amounts of data that are available to us. They will also be those who can paint the big picture for workers, encourage them, advise them, coach them, and otherwise leave them alone.

Pyramid or Spiderweb?

PC/Computing says the organization of tomorrow is going to resemble a spider's web more than the traditional hierarchical pyramid. According to the magazine, we and our computers are more likely to form part of a web, busily spinning new connections with others rather than resting as a fixed block in a pyramid.[7]

What this means to us is that we are going to have to become a lot more independent, able to function on our own without much direction from others. We are also going to have to be productive and results-oriented. When our work is moved back and forth on networks, available for scrutiny by our peers, our staffs, and our managers, we can't hide behind promises of performance. We have to deliver.

---

[7]Gareth Morgan and Wayne Tebb, "Under New Management," *PC/Computing* (October 1989), 106–110.

Key Points and Action Items

1. The corporation is being reinvented from the bottom up. A bureaucratic, controlling organization cannot survive in a world in which employees value freedom and independence more than security and certainty.

2. The PepsiCo model is a good one to follow: Take eagles and teach them to fly in formation. Use information as a tool of freedom, not an instrument of control.

3. Avoid committee structures. In an empowered organization, they are viewed as "dark alleys up which ideas are taken to be strangled."

4. Use the power of technology to flatten hierarchies and get information from the front lines to the executive suite while it is still fresh enough to influence action plans.

5. Make sure that you and everyone with whom you work understands the company's vision and mission and where you fit into it. Use the power of technology to make informed decisions and take decisive action.

7

The Electronic Generation

The future never just happened. It was created.

—WILL AND ARIEL DURANT

When Merrilee and I work in our home office, the children often stop by to chat about the events of the day or to help out with general office work. At eleven years of age, Amy and Betsy are old enough to help with filing, stuffing envelopes, and the like, and Joseph's paraphernalia—first his playpen and later his toys—have been a fixture in the office since he was born.

Recently, as Joe played with his toys while we worked, he discovered the fireproof box in which we keep insurance policies, property deeds, and other important papers along with backup computer disks. On those disks reside our family budget, our checking accounts, our investments, and every book, article, and speech I have written during the past few years.

Preoccupied with our work, neither Merrilee nor I realized what Joe was doing until he approached her desk, saying "choo-choo," and attempted to insert a disk into the computer. I had already started to reprimand him when I realized that he was using his toddler's vocabulary to tell his mother he wanted to play "Math Rabbit," a mathematics skill build-

91

ing game produced by The Learning Corporation.

At one and one-half years of age, he is far too young to play the game. All he knows is that at a certain point (when the problems are solved correctly) a choo-choo train arrives and drives the numbers off the screen. That's the part he likes.

What fascinated me was that in the box were two types of disks—the five-inch floppies that we used in our first computer, and the three-and-a-half-inch type that we use in our newer Apple Macintosh. We still use the old Tandy for some word-processing chores (at seven years of age, it's a dinosaur in the fast-paced computer world) and the kids play computer games on it.

Joe knew that the five-inch disk fit the computer at his mother's desk, and that it was the right size for the game he wanted to play. I was struck by the realization that in his world—surrounded by technology—it will be far easier for him to learn new technologies than it was for his father. I was thirty-three years old when Steve Jobs and Steve Wozniak introduced the circuit board that changed the world, and over forty when I bought my first home computer.

Transparent Technology

Perhaps it will be Joe's generation that fulfills Apple CEO John Sculley's dream of making the technology transparent to the users so that they may focus exclusively on its applications. Unconstrained by the attitudes and opinions that influenced previous generations, they will view technology as simply another tool to be applied in pursuit of an objective.

Is it possible to overrate the importance of the computer in our lives? *Scientific American* doesn't think so. In a special issue devoted to the topic, writer Michael L. Dertouzos writes: "The agricultural age was based on plows and the animals that pulled them; the industrial age on engines and the fuels that fed them. The information age that we are now creating will be based on computers and the networks that interconnect them."[1]

---

[1] Michael L. Dertouzos, "Communications, Computers and Networks, *Scientific American* (September 1991), 63, 66.

Building the Infrastructure

The consolidation, downsizing, reorganization, and intense competition we have seen in the computer industry in recent years signify the passage of the computer industry into maturity. It is growing up. *Scientific American* figures that the computer industry is about where the automobile was in the early 1900s. Until a proper infrastructure was built, travel was tedious and difficult.

The same holds true with the computer. Knowledge navigators of the future will not be constrained by primitive machines and networks any more than sixteen-year-olds learning to drive today will be limited by poor roads or nonexistent roadside service stations, restaurants, and motels. They won't give technology a second thought.

It's not just computers. For several years I conducted a seminar for business types on effective speaking skills. Participants ranged from top level executives to recent college graduates; the common denominator was that they each had jobs that often required them to make speeches or business presentations.

Reactions to Technology

The contrasts between older and younger people were dramatic. In addition to the conservatism that usually comes with age, older participants were self-conscious and camera shy. Until they began to realize the benefits of literally "seeing yourself as others see you," they hated watching their performances on video.

Most of the younger people, on the other hand, loved it. They helped run the camera, sound equipment and VCR, and when it was their turn to perform, they were likely to belt out a few bars of a popular song while we adjusted the camera. They were anything but shy.

They were equally comfortable with videoconferencing. When videoconferencing technology advanced and costs lowered sufficiently to attract widespread use, older workers had to be persuaded and sometimes trained to participate while twenty- and thirty-year-olds adjusted to the new technology as quickly as they learned a new video game.

A Faster, Global Game

In our globally competitive world, innovative companies will more and more turn to videoconferencing, electronic mail, and other technology-based devices to aid communication. It's not just the hassle and expense of travel. It's the speed. Videoconferences can be held, problems solved, and agreement reached before participants can get their airline boarding passes on their way to a central location for a face-to-face meeting.

Videoconferencing has even sneaked into corporate boardrooms. According to *Fortune* magazine, many outside directors don't even go to meetings any longer. They participate via video or teleconference calls.

Citing a study by the executive search firm Korn/Ferry International, the magazine reports that of 426 Fortune 500 industrial and 500 service companies that responded to a survey by the headhunters, ''315 firms paid outside directors to attend board meetings electronically at least once a year.''[2]

Videoconferencing saves time and travel costs, and it also allows us to participate in events that would logistically be impossible otherwise. Major meetings can be broadcast live to the entire organization, new products can be introduced, and buyers for retail stores can review the latest fashions and make purchasing decisions via videoconferencing.

In the automotive industry, far-flung dealerships conduct training programs, learn about new products, problems, and company policies on regular satellite television broadcasts beamed at them. There is even an Automotive Satellite Television Network that covers industry news in daily broadcasts to auto dealers.

Although videoconferences are replacing face-to-face meetings in many companies, and are regularly used for training, roundtable discussions, technical project reviews, and even depositions in civil lawsuits, improved technology may soon make obsolete the dedicated videoconference room.

---

[2] ''Directors: 'Beam Me Up, Scotty,' '' *Fortune* (April 23, 1990), 18.

Desktop Videoconferencing Hardware

Today's videoconference facilities with television monitors, multiple cameras (for televising people and graphics), control panels, VCRs, slide projectors, and computer hookups may soon give way to compact systems that capitalize on lower costs and recent advances in computer chip, audio and video compression, and networking technology.

The technology already exists to turn your personal computer into a picture phone, and several manufacturers have begun to introduce the hardware that makes it possible. Such systems will allow you to work on one side of the screen while viewing the person to whom you are talking on the other side. Just remember not to wear your bathrobe when you are talking to the office.

Musical Technology

Information technology is affecting our lives in ways that most of us don't even realize. In the music business, for example, modern studios use computers to create sound, and synchronize, synthesize, and enhance it until the recording you hear is almost perfect. Digitized recordings allow technicians to coordinate perfectly an infinite variety of instruments playing the right notes at precisely the same time. If a song sounds too good to be true, it may be. The sounds that come together in your CD player may never have existed outside of a computer's memory.

Computers are used to create visuals, animate cartoons, run laser shows, and choreograph special effects. Songwriter and rock singer Leon Russell, whose "Jumpin' Jack Flash" became a Rolling Stones hit, performs from a special movable platform that is equipped with his keyboard and an array of supporting electronic paraphernalia.

A personal computer mounted on either side of the keyboard is his electronic equivalent of sheet music. The computer on his right contains the entire show, including encores, while the one on the left displays the lyrics. Atop the keyboard is a track ball that allows him to scroll through the songs or otherwise move information around as he wishes during the performance. The technology ensures that he never misses a beat as he belts out ''Jumpin' Jack Flash,'' ''Queen of the Roller Derby,'' or ''Roll in My Sweet Baby's Arms'' at a sound level slightly below a decibel in the range of bodily injury or property damage.

High-Tech Restaurants

Even restaurants have gone high-tech. In addition to pots and pans, furniture, stoves and other cooking equipment, the assets of your favorite trendy restaurant probably include computers, copiers, printers, fax machines, and computerized cash registers. Technology is used to keep books, pay bills, write checks, design menus, and print promotional pieces.

Daily specials can be quickly printed, eliminating the need for food servers to spend time memorizing and reciting specials or explaining how exotic dishes are made. Greg and Sally Morton, proprietors of the twenty-five-table Bridge Street Cafe in the harbor village of Padanaram, Massachusetts, even use computer-generated pieces to promote sales of profitable specialty items and they publish a newsletter that is mailed to about fifteen hundred customers, friends, and prospective customers in surrounding towns. They use it to promote membership in their lunch club and to tout upcoming promotional events.

''The restaurant business is a labor-intensive, low-margin one, made more difficult because restauranteurs are at once manufacturers, retailers, and service providers. For the business to succeed, the product must be good, the location accessible and inviting, the service excellent. That's a tall order for any business owner. But computers lend a critical helping hand. 'The computers,' says Greg, 'let us do something we never could have done before—run a nice little family business.' ''[3]

Changing Reading Habits

In the publishing world, it has long been recognized that there is one class of reader that has been little influenced by

---

[3]Nick Sullivan, ''Technology Comes to Rescue of Seaside Cafe,'' *Home-Office Computing* (May 1991), 58–59.

technology: commuters. On every subway, bus, and train that shuttles workers from their homes in the suburbs to their offices in the city, readers are ubiquitous. In particularly crowded areas such as New York, they have established social customs. It's customary, for example, to fold newspapers into quarters in order not to intrude into your seatmate's limited airspace. Violation of this custom is at your own peril.

People find innovative ways to use commuting time constructively, perhaps to rationalize the decision to live far from work. As a regular rider of the Chicago and North Western Railroad years ago, I got an emotional boost from a couple who rode my usual evening train. Though they were obviously middle-aged, they were clearly still very much in love and demonstrated it to any who cared to observe by frequent caresses and kisses.

One day I rode beyond my usual stop to meet some friends for dinner and watched them get off the train—at separate stops—to be met by their spouses. Apparently they had been having an affair for years, meeting mostly on the train.

Legend has it that Chicago attorney Scott Turow wrote his best-selling *Presumed Innocent* on a yellow legal pad as he commuted in and out of the city.

Most, however, amused themselves by reading. Over the years, though, the character of commuters began to change. Walkmans and CD players with headphones began to replace newspapers and magazines. Now, according to recent news reports, the printed page may be another step closer to being replaced by its electronic counterpart.

The Electronic Newspaper

Newsweek points out that these days most books and magazines start out on computer screens and asks the question: "So why not just eliminate the messy business with ink and save some trees?"[4] The day is not far away, experts predict, when we will be able to do just that. We will be able to receive satellite transmissions of our daily newspaper or our favorite television shows, and we can send electronic mail and faxes—

---

[4]Michael Rogers, "The Literary Circuit-ry," *Newsweek* (June 29, 1992), 66.

all on our portable laptop computers. We may even be able to "blend text and video so that a user could watch a segment from the evening news and read an accompanying story."[5]

Much of the renewed interest in electronic publishing on the part of newspapers is the result of two factors. First is a legal decision that allowed telephone companies to become information providers, a ruling which effectively places them in competition with the news media.

Second, the technology has advanced to the point that the quality of laptop computer presentation is expected to be comparable to that of a printed page within the next couple of years. In addition, the same digital transmission capabilities that are advancing videoconferencing will allow for economical transmission of electronic newspapers.

Most major newspaper companies are now seriously examining electronic publishing as an option, and books are already available on computers. One day in the not too distant future, we may be able to go into our corner bookstore, buy our favorite novelist's latest offering on a computer disk, and stuff it into our beach bag along with our towel, suntan lotion, and laptop computer.

The Technological Revolution

Such technological advances may revolutionize society as did Gutenberg's printing press some five and one-half centuries ago. For the first time, information that had been restricted to the socially and intellectually elite became available to the masses. Great advances in civilization were made simply because the grand thoughts of one generation could be stored in printed form for the next generation to discover. Knowledge expanded exponentially.

When and if all these technologies are linked together, the electronic cottage may well allow us to work and play for days on end without ever talking to another human being. We can easily commute to work thousands of miles—even internationally—electronically. Social skills will become rusty and

[5]John Markoff, "A Media Pioneer's Quest: Portable Electronic Newspapers," *New York Times*, 28 June 1992, 11.

salesmanship may be far more dependent on the ability to craft a persuasive electronic message accompanied by a short product video than on the ability to stir a prospect's emotions in an eyeball-to-eyeball selling situation.

Different Values

When the electronic generation assumes its leadership role in corporations, government, the professions, and society, traditional motivators such as peer pressure, competitiveness, and the endless search for personal wealth may be replaced by a quest for individual freedom, selective teamwork, and the constant search for knowledge.

We are already seeing the leading edge of this movement. William H. Gates III, the billionaire founder of Microsoft Corporation, for years bought most of his clothes at K-mart, and the vast majority of the more than four hundred millionaires who work for him (most of them under thirty years of age) have not even bought a house.

Their values are different. Most are tekkies who write software, not typical executives. They seldom contribute to politicians, established charities, benefits, or the arts. The principal difference between this group and others who got rich in other ventures, according to the *New York Times*, is that the Microsoft millionaires "came for the dream, not the pay."[6]

A New Mission

The Microsoft millionaires are on a mission. Like many other members of the electronic generation, they see technology as an opportunity to change the world. When the next phase of the electronics revolution unfolds, they will be there—waving the flag and leading the charge.

Tomorrow's senior executives have little use for office politics and they are impatient with traditional corporate hierarchies. They are brash and irreverent, and they aren't willing to work sixty- to eighty-hour weeks and blindly follow orders to get to the top. They question conventional wisdom, and

[6]Timothy Egan, "Microsoft's Unlikely Millionaires," *New York Times*, 28 June 1992, Sec. 3, 1.

require less social interaction than their predecessors. They are perfectly comfortable with a paperless society; they buy, bank, and work with a computer.

To be successful in such an environment requires great flexibility, self-confidence, and the ability to motivate and entertain yourself. The "brave new world" is coming. Prepare yourself.

Key Points and Action Items

1. It is impossible to overrate the importance of the computer. Just as the industrial age was based on engines and fuels that fed them, the information age we are creating will be built upon computers and the networks that interconnect them.

2. The computer today is at about the stage the automobile was in the early 1900s. When the infrastructure linking technologies is in place, we will see quantum advances. Be ready, or be left behind.

3. Great competitive advantages will accrue to those who learn to use the technology that is available in today's fast-paced, global economy.

4. The ability to profit from new technologies is all around us. We are constrained only by our imaginations in developing new applications for them.

5. The technological revolution will continue to have a profound influence upon our society and values. We will have less social interaction, we will work alone more, and we will have to find new ways to motivate ourselves and our employees.

8

External Forces You Can't Control

It isn't so much that hard times are coming; the change observed is mostly soft times going.

—GROUCHO MARX

It is possible to get a proper education, work hard, and have the right attitude—to do everything correctly to the best of your ability—and still have everything fall apart? You bet it is. Random events, over which you have little or no control, may suddenly change your life forever. Here is an example from personal experience.

In the summer of 1990, I was on top of the world. I was director of communications for KPMG Peat Marwick, then the world's largest professional services firm. If one believed the experts who said the U.S. was in the process of transforming itself from its traditional manufacturing base into a service economy, I arguably had the best job in my field. I occupied the top communications post in the world's largest professional services firm.

As an extension of my regular work, I had agreed to write a book about the 1987 merger between the big eight accounting and consulting firm Peat Marwick, Mitchell & Co. and the European firm Klynveld Main Goerdeler. At the time, it was the largest merger of its type ever undertaken and in the low-key, green eyeshades world of professional accounting, there was a good deal of interest in the inside story of how the merger was orchestrated.

I had spent a year traveling the world, interviewing key participants in merger talks, and conducting research for the book. In the process, I had gotten to know many of the top officials of the firm. Larry Horner, chairman of both the U.S. and international organizations, enthusiastically supported the book project and made himself available to answer questions at any time. I was greatly chagrined when I awakened him on a Saturday morning after he had taken the red-eye flight from Los Angeles to New York, but he was gracious and answered my questions so I could finish the chapter I was writing.

Jim Butler, the chairman of the U.K. firm (who is now chairman of the worldwide organization), a British gentleman in every respect, picked me up at the airport and lent me his automobile and chauffeur when tight schedules made it difficult to make meetings with senior partners in the firm. In addition, the organization had committed a six-figure budget to advertise and promote the book.

The point of all this nostalgia is that I felt very secure in my position. I was known and respected by the senior partners in the firm and had a staff of dependable, quality people capable of running the department while I traveled. Life was good.

Upside-Down World

Suddenly everything changed. When the partners questioned his choice for deputy chairman, Larry Horner decided not to seek another term as chairman and retired to pursue other opportunities and interests in investments and on corporate boards. In what the newspapers referred to as a coup d'état, Jon Madonna, the managing partner of the San Francisco office, was elected to the post of chairman. He was an "outsider" candidate who had spent his entire career with the firm in San Francisco and had little use for the status quo or the people he connected with it.

In the space of a few weeks, I had fallen from the top to

the bottom. I had entered a management twilight zone. What had been good before was now bad, and what was bad before was now good. I very quickly learned that if I thought it was a swell idea, Madonna wouldn't like it. If I thought it was dumb, he would love it. It seemed to me that the only thing we agreed upon was that we didn't agree about anything. The handwriting was on the wall in big red letters. When my boss and mentor—who was Madonna's successful campaign manager—submitted his resignation, I knew my time had come.

Fortunately, unlike many others in similar positions in the midst of a recession, I had other options. The most promising was Masco Corporation, a Taylor (near Detroit), Michigan-based Fortune 200 manufacturer of products for the home and family. The country's largest manufacturer of faucets, kitchen cabinets, and furniture, Masco's brand names—Delta and Peerless faucets; Merillat, Kraft Maid, Starmark, and Fieldstone cabinetry; and Henredon, Drexel Heritage, Lexington, and Universal furniture—are among the best known in the business.

I met Masco through Dave Kinsella, with whom I had worked in Chicago several years earlier. When he joined Masco as Director of Executive Search, one of his first assignments was to recruit a director of communications. I had talked with Masco about the position for three years, but the timing had not been right. Once I was writing the KPMG book and didn't want to leave it unfinished; another time, my daughter Amy was hospitalized for a long period and I thought it would be unwise to move until she had recovered.

The Right Time for a Change

With the situation at Peat Marwick deteriorating daily, the time was right. I wrote Kinsella and advised him that I was leaving and asked him to keep me in mind for any positions that he might know about. I had not talked to him for some time, and I fully expected that the Masco job had been filled. I later learned he took my letter to John Nicholls, my boss today, and said, "See, I told you we would get him eventually." John said, "Call him and tell him not to go anywhere until he talks to us."

I was on the next flight to Detroit and accepted Masco's

offer as soon as it was extended. The Peat Marwick revolution occurred in early October; I started my new job December 18. I had landed a better position with a better compensation package with a company that obviously cares about its employees. They had allowed me to wait until the timing was right for me.

Before you get the idea that I think I'm pretty clever about such career moves, let me quickly squelch any such notions. I think I was extremely fortunate, if not downright lucky, to find the right circumstances and the help of some very good people at the right time. I had, however, done one thing right. Over the years, I had kept my options open.

Maintain Your Network

Maintaining your network is one the best ways to protect yourself when companies reorganize, cut staff, or lay off employees because of economic conditions, according to Donald F. Dvorak who heads up his own executive search consulting practice in the affluent Chicago suburb of Wilmette, Illinois. "Unfortunately," he told Merrilee in a recent telephone interview, "it's too late for you to begin your job search after the axe has fallen. What you should have been doing all along is developing professional visibility for yourself because you have the beginnings of your network already in place.

"People who have never taken the time to become active in any professional or business association, to maintain alumni relations with their college, or to write or speak in a way to indirectly advertise themselves, are really starting from a cold, extraordinarily difficult position," Dvorak says.

It takes time to find a new job at a comparable salary level. While contemporary executive search professionals discount the cracker-barrel philosophy that it requires at least a month to replace every $10,000 in salary, finding a new job takes time and the higher you were in the organization, the longer it is likely to be before you find a similar position elsewhere. There are only five hundred CEOs of Fortune 500 companies, for example, and it's a pretty safe assumption that most of the incumbents in those positions would like to stay where they are.

Everyone Is Vulnerable

"Unfortunately, in this country because of the many cut-backs that have occurred in industry," Dvorak notes, "there are many people who have never thought of having to go out and look for another job. Suddenly, after twenty years, they find themselves thrust into an environment that they are totally unequipped to deal with. They have no preparation whatso-ever. They don't know what a résumé looks like, don't know what to do with it, and don't know how to present themselves. They haven't been interviewed in twenty-five years, and don't recognize what an interview is."

Dvorak believes the worst mistake you can make is to as-sume that the interviewer is skilled at asking the right ques-tions to determine your strengths and weaknesses. Most managers interview prospective employees infrequently, at most, and are not very good at it. If you are the person being interviewed, you need to have a clear fix on your strongest selling points and to be able to deftly steer the conversation into areas that will help you market yourself.

Most of us wouldn't consider trying to sell a commercial product or service without knowing as much as possible about it and having a strong marketing plan that effectively dem-onstrates its features and benefits to prospective customers. Yet when it comes to selling our most important product— ourselves—we assume the marketing will somehow take care of itself. Others will immediately recognize our intrinsic worth.

Forget the Past

If you find yourself in a situation where you've lost your job through no fault of your own or because of a conflict of some kind, Dvorak says the first step you must take to get your life together is to depart the organization mentally. Put it behind you. Don't spend your time agonizing about what happened and what you might have done to prevent its hap-pening. It's a natural human reaction to try to "work yourself back into the job instead of saying, 'I am not here any longer. What do I do now to begin my life anew?' " Dvorak says.

The only thing that matters about your old job at this point is what your former employer is going to say to prospective new employers concerning the reason for your departure. Make sure you have a clear understanding about what will be said.

Ironically, you may be in a pretty good negotiating position. Most bosses hate firing someone, and if you are professional and unemotional in your acceptance of the inevitable, they may be willing to give you a letter of recommendation and more favorable severance terms than they would have been if you were hostile or accusatory. When you are being told, it's too late to renegotiate the past; the decision has been made and approved up the line. Your goal at this point should be to get the best possible terms and conditions of separation. All they can do is say "no" if you ask for more severance pay, benefits continuation, outplacement assistance, and secretarial service until you find a new job.

Focus on Your New Priorities

After the break has been made, your first new job is to get a job. You should be totally focused on your next position. You may have been the right person in your old job when you began it, but as time passed, things were no longer the same. The business changed, competition or regulation altered the business, or the skills the organization required were changed.

Maybe you were unable or unwilling to change or maybe the organization did indeed fail you. Perhaps it was unable to develop people to allow them to grow and become effective in a new environment. It doesn't matter. The facts are the same. You are no longer there.

You should begin immediately to develop an active job search program for yourself. Dvorak advises that you begin by assessing your skills and abilities as you would if you were evaluating a product that is going to market. If you have trouble objectively analyzing your pluses and minuses, you may need help from an outplacement firm. Because of the massive changes that have gone on in business in recent years, there are many such firms from which to choose.

In addition to helping you analyze your "product," outplacement firms provide emotional support and professional advice about résumés, interviews, consulting opportunities, and working your network. "There is no substitute for networking," Dvorak says. "Executive recruiters are not the only answer. I often tell people that I am the last of their answers, not the first, and represent only about ten percent of the effort needed in finding a new job. The other ninety percent should be directed toward their network."

Help When You Least Expect It

You never know from what source help may come. When Merrilee and I were first married, I was "between engagements" and struggling to support myself as a free-lance writer while I looked for a job. One day I got a phone call from a friend I had made at a journalism society meeting inviting me to lunch. I had not seen him in over a year, but his wife saw my wedding picture in the local newspaper and remembered his mentioning my name on occasion.

Over lunch, he told me about an open position at his company, one that matched my background and experience. He introduced me to the right people, and in a matter of days I was on the payroll. If my personal marketing plan had included the possibility that a friend's wife who had never met me would see my wedding photo in the local newspaper, remember to mention it to her husband, and that he would take the time and trouble to track me down, any rational person (myself included) would have thought I was nuts. But, that's how networking works; a friend of a friend of a friend hears about an opportunity somewhere, and something eventually works out.

Timing and Luck

When I was in college, I had the opportunity to meet Dr. Ernest Dale, author of the textbook we studied in a principles of management class. At Southwestern Oklahoma State University, out on the windswept prairie, that was a big deal. We didn't often get to meet the people behind the words.

I asked Dr. Dale a question that I would ask many other achievers in succeeding years: If you had to identify one reason why some people succeed while others fail, what would it be? He thoughtfully replied, "Well, of course, you have to have the right qualifications—education, experience, and the like—and you must have persistence. You cannot give up if you don't reach your goal the first time. But, there are often many determined people with very similar backgrounds striving for the same goal. I must tell you that the older I get, the more I realize that luck—being in the right place at the right time with the right credentials—has more to do with success than anything else.''

As we talked, I gradually realized what he was telling me was that there will always be circumstances in your life and career that you cannot control. You cannot manage events; you can only manage your reaction to them. When you fail at something through no fault of your own, you can accept defeat and give up, or you can learn from the experience and refocus your energies in a direction that will ultimately lead to success. As Texas Longhorns' coach Darrell Royal once observed, luck is what happens when preparation meets opportunity.

The Kentucky Colonel

Soon after my conversation with Dr. Dale, I had the good luck to meet Harland Sanders, the legendary Kentucky Fried Chicken Colonel whose reaction to uncontrollable events helped launch the $25 billion fast-food industry in America. He was almost eighty years old at the time and traveling a quarter of a million miles a year making public appearances and visiting his KFC empire.

What impressed me most about Colonel Sanders was his outlook on life, his ability to cope with change. He was born in 1890, five years after the invention of the automobile, eighteen years before Wilbur and Orville Wright made their historic flight at Kitty Hawk, North Carolina, and more than three-quarters of a century before Alan Shepard became the first American in space. Yet, Colonel Sanders not only changed with the times, he helped create the changes.

Harland Sanders got his first job—as a farmhand—at ten years of age. At fifteen, he was a streetcar conductor in New Albany, Indiana, and at sixteen he served as a private in the U.S. Army in Cuba. He was a railroad fireman, studied law by correspondence, practiced in justice of the peace courts, sold insurance, operated an Ohio River steamboat ferry, sold tires, and ran a service station.

When he was forty, he started cooking for travelers who stopped at his service station in Corbin, Kentucky. He didn't even have a restaurant; he just invited people into his own dining room in the living quarters of the service station.

Word spread, and more people came. He moved across the street to a motel and 142-seat restaurant. His fame grew. He attended Cornell University's elite restaurant school, the governor named him a Kentucky Colonel (in recognition of his contributions to the state's cuisine), and his restaurant was known far and wide for the fried chicken he made with his own secret blend of eleven herbs and spices.

Sixty-five and Broke

Suddenly, things changed. A new interstate highway that was to bypass the town of Corbin sounded the death knell for Sanders's business. He auctioned off his operations, paid his bills, and took stock of himself. He was sixty-five years old and broke, reduced to living on his $105 monthly social security check.

What he did have, though, was his famous recipe and a strong belief in himself. He hit the road in his old car, traveling from restaurant to restaurant, cooking chicken for restaurant owners and employees. If they liked the chicken, he made a handshake agreement that the restaurant would pay him a nickel for every chicken it sold.

Ten years later Colonel Sanders had more than 600 franchised outlets for his chicken in the U.S. and Canada. He sold his interest in the U.S. company for $2 million to a group of investors that included John Y. Brown, Jr., who sixteen years later was elected governor of Kentucky.

The Colonel stayed on with the company, visiting restaurants, making public appearances, and opening new stores until he died of leukemia in 1980 at the age of ninety. The investors took the company public, and sold it to Heublein Inc. in 1971 for $285 million. KFC Corporation became a part of R.J. Reynolds (now RJR Nabisco) when Heublein was acquired by Reynolds in 1982. In 1986 PepsiCo bought KFC from RJR Nabisco for about $840 million.

Last year, close to three billion of the Colonel's "finger lickin' good" chicken dinners—about ten pieces for every man, woman, and child in America—were served in this country. KFC Corporation posted worldwide sales in 1991 of $2 billion through six thousand franchises and company owned stores in fifty-four countries. Today, the company, which was born when a sixty-five-year-old Kentucky gentleman found an opportunity in the external forces that put him out of business, employs 500,000 people around the world.

Lemons into Lemonade

Another who figured out how to turn lemons into lemonade is Marilyn Marks. When Dorsey Trailers, her Atlanta-based truck trailer company was struck by a tornado and a flood within the same month, she saved the company by persuading the Small Business Administration to give her and her eleven partners (she owns fifty percent of the company) a low interest $25 million loan—the largest in SBA history.

A tough-minded entrepreneur with a background in accounting, Marks led the 1987 management buyout of Dorsey Trailers. At the time, she was a vice president of Constar International, Dorsey's parent company. When her boss assigned to her the task of finding a buyer for the Dorsey division, she recognized its potential and raised the capital to buy the company herself.

Disaster Strikes

The company was well on its way to tapping the potential she saw in Dorsey, building sales nearly forty percent in two years to $180 million in 1990, when disaster struck the company's key operations in Elba, Alabama. Sixteen inches of rain in forty-eight hours weakened a levee on the nearby Pea River and within three hours, the plant was under ten feet of water.

All the company's files and its mainframe computer were destroyed, sensitive machinery and equipment were underwater, and hundreds of gallons of industrial chemicals were floating around the plant. "I flew there as soon as I heard," Marks said. "The sheriff rode me through the streets in a motorboat to see our plant, and I had to duck to keep from being hit by traffic lights."

Marks set up temporary headquarters in a nearby hotel room, where she and her management team directed disaster relief efforts, tracking down food, potable water, and tetanus serum for workers involved in the effort, paying employees and vendors with checks they printed with two computers salvaged from the plant.

Although the plant and equipment were insured, under the terms of the buyout all the insurance proceeds were used to liquidate loans. Marks knew she had to find financing to keep the company afloat, something she and her partners were committed to doing. Dorsey is a major employer in Elba, providing jobs to seven hundred of the town's forty-four hundred residents, a fact that was not lost on the SBA.

To help employees get through the trauma caused by the events, they arranged for state and federal government counseling, assistance she describes as having "a very positive influence." Such concern for the employees would pay off later. Workers, many of whom lost their homes in the flood, were thankful that their jobs were saved. They agreed to a two percent wage cut to help get the company back in operation with new, more efficient equipment. Dorsey was in limited production within three months after the flood.

Marks shares the conviction of many of her employees that the company is stronger as a result of the adversity it has faced. "We've weathered Mother Nature, a recession, and a slowdown in the industry," she says. "We can't be beaten."

Why Me?

When we are the victim of such events, the natural inclination is to ask: Why me? As rational people, we try to find logic in an illogical situation. We try to make sense out of events that make no sense. Harold S. Kushner said that the philosophical basis of his best-selling book *When Bad Things Happen to Good People* is the idea that some things happen for no reason.

"Some people cannot handle the idea," he writes. "They look for connections, striving desperately to make sense of all that happens. They convince themselves that God is cruel, or that they are sinners, rather than accept randomness. Sometimes, when they have made sense of ninety percent of everything they know, they let themselves assume that the other ten percent makes sense also, but lies beyond the reach of their understanding. But why do we have to insist on everything being reasonable? Why must everything happen for a specific reason? Why can't we let the universe have a few rough edges?''

Kushner concludes that it is possible that ''God finished his work of creating eons ago, and left the rest to us. Residual chaos, chance and mischance, things happening for no reason, will continue to be with us ... We will simply have to learn to live with it, sustained and comforted by the knowledge that the earthquake and the accident, like the murder and the robbery, are not the will of God, but represent that aspect of reality which stands independent of His will, and which angers and saddens God even as it angers and saddens us.''[1]

Finding Our Own Answers

It may well be that if any good is to come out of a bad situation, it is up to us to make it happen. When Betty Ford became one of the country's most high-profile alcohol and prescription drug abusers, she started a clinic to help others with the same problem. Today, she is a recovering alcoholic and the Betty Ford Center in Rancho Mirage, California, has helped thousands of others to take control of their lives.

When we deal with any problem in our lives—facing up to an addiction, a job loss, death of a loved one, or illness—the experts tell us that we will inevitably go through a predictable process. In the best-seller *Life 101*, John-Roger and Peter McWilliams write:

''There are three distinct, yet overlapping phases of recovery. We go through each phase no matter what the loss. The only difference is intensity of feeling, and duration. In a minor loss, we can experience all three stages in a few minutes. In a major loss, the recovery process can take years.''[2]

---

[1]Harold S. Kushner, *When Bad Things Happen to Good People* (New York: Avon Books, 1981), 46, 55.
[2]John-Roger and Peter McWilliams, *Life 101* (Los Angeles: Prelude Press, 1991), 131.

Dealing with Loss

The first stage the authors identify is shock/denial. We are so overwhelmed by the magnitude of events that we at first refuse to accept our loss. We feel numb.

The second stage is anger/depression. We may know intellectually that becoming angry will not help the situation, but we cannot control our emotions. We are angry at the cause of the loss; we sometimes even become angry with the person who was insensitive enough to leave us—even though he or she may have died. Anger may be accompanied by depression. We feel an overwhelming sense of sadness and grief.

The third stage is understanding/acceptance. Gradually we begin to come to terms with the loss and realize that life goes on. We retain the happy memories of the person or thing we have lost and we grow as people as a result of having gone through the experience.

Betty Ford found that accepting the fact that she had a problem—despite her vigorous denial at first—put her back in control of her life. "When I was a practicing alcoholic," she told *Modern Maturity*, "my family—especially the children were very able to manipulate me. I'd say yes to practically anything. After I got into recovery I took control of my life. At first there was a lot of resentment that I suddenly wanted to be in charge again. They had to realize this was a healthy person and this was what recovery was all about."

Since she quit drinking, Ford has found healthier ways to relax after a busy day. "I find tea or a cup of coffee sort of relaxing. If I'm really tired I go swimming in our pool. I exercise. And I have some meditation books I use to regroup my thoughts. It's a matter of balance."[3]

A strong sense of "self" is essential to striking the balance required to succeed in today's crowded, intense, fast-paced world. Only when we firmly know what we're about can we deal constructively with the changes that affect our lives, our careers, and our relationships with others.

---

[3]Karen Westerberg Reyes, "Interview With Betty Ford," *Modern Maturity* (February-March 1992), 29.

Key Points and Action Items

1. It is possible to go from the top of the world to the bottom with breathtaking speed. Everyone is vulnerable. No matter how secure you feel, keep your options open.

2. Your network is still the best source of job opportunities. Stay active in your business or professional association, maintain alumni relations with your college, and subtly advertise yourself in articles and speeches.

3. Help may come from totally unexpected sources. Keep your net out and remember Coach Darrell Royal's observation: "Luck is what happens when preparation meets opportunity."

4. It's never too late to change. Colonel Harland Sanders was sixty-five and broke when he hit the road with his secret recipe and built his Kentucky Fried Chicken empire.

5. Some things are simply random, uncontrollable, and unexplainable. Don't agonize over things that make no sense. Positively manage your reaction to them.

9

Finding Your Way amid the Clutter

You miss one hundred percent of the shots you never take.

—Wayne Gretzky

Curt Carlson related a story to me several years ago that succinctly illustrates the value of having a plan for your life. As the story goes, a Yale professor asked members of a graduating class how many had written down the goal that they had set for themselves once they entered the "real world." Only three or four raised their hands. When the same class was assembled for a reunion some thirty years later, those who had raised their hands on graduation day three decades earlier had accumulated as much wealth as the rest of the class combined.

The chairman and CEO of Minneapolis-based Carlson Companies, Inc., Carlson so firmly believes in planning and goal setting that he has institutionalized the process in his company. A $9.3 billion marketing, travel, and hospitality giant, Carlson Companies is one of America's largest privately owned corporations, and Curt Carlson is one of the country's wealthiest entrepreneurs. His holdings include Carlson Hospitality Group, composed of Radisson Hotels International, Colony Hotels & Resorts, TGI Friday's, and a number of other restaurant chains; Carlson Marketing Group, the world's largest marketing agency, which numbers most of the Fortune 500 among its clients; and Carlson Travel Group, one of the world's largest travel management companies.

Being the Best

Indeed, goal setting and accountability provide the foundation on which Carlson Companies is built. Elegant, gold-embossed company literature reminds readers in plain language that despite the size and international scope of Carlson Companies, it remains committed to the principles upon which it was founded—entrepreneurial initiative, goal setting, and excellence of performance—with the objective of being the best in each of its businesses. In a world of fuzzy, imprecise corporate mission statements, Carlson Companies knows exactly what it is about and where it is going.

The no-nonsense statement of purpose is deeply rooted in the chairman's character. He built the company by setting realistic goals and a timetable for their achievement, telling everyone in the organization about them, and refusing to give up until they were reached. When he founded the company—and was its only employee—he wrote his goal on a little piece of paper that he carried around in his wallet.

He carried it, he says, so it would become a part of him and become crystallized in his mind. Setting goals helped him establish priorities that guided him during the daily crush of business activities. With a written goal that spelled out exactly what he planned to achieve, decisions were easier. Either the action would move him closer to his goal or it would move him farther away from it. When he reached a goal, he would remove the frayed and dog-eared piece of paper on which it was written and replace it with another, this one inscribed with a new, more ambitious goal.

Classic Success Story

Carlson's is one of the classic success stories of the American free enterprise system. He founded the Gold Bond Stamp Company in his hometown of Minneapolis in 1938 at the height of the Great Depression. He began with an idea, a mail drop, and $50 in borrowed capital. His trading stamp idea to promote grocery sales proved popular with consumers and very quickly swept the country. All over America, housewives pasted Gold Bond Stamps in books provided by merchants that could be redeemed for merchandise and other premiums.

The Great Depression was hardly over when adversity struck again. Food rationing during World War II limited the appeal of trading stamps and Carlson had to streamline operations to survive. Despite the difficulties in its early days, the company grew at a compounded rate of thirty-three percent annually during the first four decades, and has doubled its revenues every five years since 1973.

In the 1950s, Carlson got a big break when he sold his first major supermarket chain. He quickly replicated his success in the grocery business using the same techniques to sell the Gold Bond Stamp program to service stations and dry cleaners, retailers whose success hinged on customer loyalty. When the consumerist movement of the 1960s shifted the focus to lower supermarket prices and away from premiums and promotions, Carlson diversified.

He entered the hotel business in 1962 with the purchase of the original Radisson Hotel in downtown Minneapolis. It was the genesis of the hospitality business which today boasts over 300 major hotels, inns, and resorts around the world. Ever flexible and alert for synergistic opportunities, Carlson acquired Dallas-based TGI Friday's in 1975; the company now owns two hundred of the restaurants, a number that it expects to double by 1996. Entering the travel business in 1979 with the purchase of Ask Mr. Foster agencies, Carlson Travel Group now numbers two thousand agencies, and is adding new ones at the rate of thirty per month.

Ambitious Goals

Doubling the company's sales every five years is certainly no small feat, and it is no accident. Managers are given a bogey of an annual increase in sales of fifteen percent, rain or shine, in good times or bad. Compounded, the fifteen percent yearly increase neatly adds up to a one hundred percent increase in five years time.

In the mid-1980s, when we were researching *Believe and*

Achieve, Carlson told us that he had a sign in the lobby to remind all employees when they entered the building that the company's goal was to achieve $4 billion in sales in 1987. By my calculations, that meant Carlson Companies should be reaching $8 billion in sales by the end of 1992. I wondered if he had revised his goals downward as many companies did when business was buffeted by the Persian Gulf war and the protracted recession in the early 1990s.

He had indeed revised his projections, but instead of lowering them, he'd raised them! As others in travel and hospitality struggled during the downturn and complained about bad business conditions, Carlson told his executives, "Don't worry about the economy and the recession. There is plenty of business out there for us so let's not blame the marketplace for any sales problems."

Carlson Companies passed the $8 billion mark in 1990 and posted systemwide revenues of $9.9 billion for the service year 1992. At this writing, Carlson is projecting sales of over $10 billion for 1993. The company has so exceeded its five-year plan that at its annual sales meeting this year, Carlson told the assembled executives that he had decided to change to a three-year plan for increased sales goals instead of the five-year plan he has followed for over fifty years in his company. "I think three years is more realistic going into the nineties and the year 2000," he said. "We will simply examine our progress more often."

Despite the impressive sales growth in 1991, Carlson Companies fell short of profit expectations, particularly in the Carlson Marketing Group, which has many incentive programs tied to the Big Three automakers in Detroit. Carlson responded by making "Profits First!" the theme of his annual sales conference. With characteristic optimism and determination, he said, "We expect to get much of this business back starting in 1992 as more and more companies are transferring their advertising dollars to sales promotion and incentives—an area where we are the very best in the business."

Elements of a Goal

His approach to planning and goal setting is a model of simplicity, one that can be used by any person or organization, regardless of the size of the goal or of the company. The basic elements of his approach are:

1. Make your goal realistic. Unachievable goals demoralize people when they are unable to attain them. Eventually such goals become meaningless.

2. Be specific. Esoteric concepts such as "being the best in our industry" are too subjective and difficult to measure. When every person in the organization does his or her best every day to meet specific, achievable goals, you will be the best in the industry.

3. Break your overall goal down into small parts. Set short-, intermediate-, and long-term goals. Your annual goal, for example, should be broken down into monthly goals.

4. Set a definite timetable for achieving your overall goal as well as each of its increments.

5. Go public. Tell everyone about your goal. If you keep it to yourself, it is too easy to rationalize your failure to meet it.

6. Monitor your progress regularly and make adjustments as required to meet your goal. Don't procrastinate and expect to make up a shortfall in an unreasonable period of time.

7. Be persistent. Never give up. There will always be adversity and unforeseen circumstances. Make adjustments necessary to deal with the situation, intensify your effort, and fortify your determination.

Passing the Torch

Carlson took a brief hiatus as CEO in 1989 when his son-in-law, Edwin C. (Skip) Gage, became the chief executive and likely successor, but returned to the helm a couple of years later when he was dissatisfied with the company's performance during the recession. At seventy-seven years of age, Carlson says he has no plans to retire any time soon. He spends much of his time these days preparing his oldest daughter, Marilyn Nelson, fifty-two, to take over the top job at the company.

It is not a sure thing. Carlson has high standards for his

professional management team, and equally high standards for family members who stand to inherit the business. He told the *New York Times*, "My daughter is busy learning the business, and she has tremendous capacity, but time will tell where we are." Joining the company full-time two years ago as vice chairman of Carlson Holdings Inc., the parent of Carlson Companies, Nelson is currently in charge of the company's new customer satisfaction and quality control programs as well as the company's Carlson Travel Network credit card issued with VISA as she learns more about Carlson Companies' operations.

Company insiders give her good marks on her performance to date, but the *Times* opines that, "In the long run, what really matters is not whether others think Mrs. Nelson is qualified to run the company, but whether her father thinks so. For after Mr. Gage's departure, few think that Curt Carlson will be guided by sentiment in the matter of succession.

"Mrs. Nelson certainly does not. 'I understand to the depths of my being what this company means to Curt,' she said in a recent interview. 'This is his child, and he couldn't stop being its parent any more than I could stop being my kids' mom.' "[1]

Is it possible to sustain this kind of growth indefinitely? Probably not. Eventually a company reaches a point where the dollar volume required to achieve a fifteen percent increase is staggering, and each market share increase requires costly, sustained battles with competitors. But Carlson has consistently beaten the odds with his planning and goal-setting approach and a tough management style that holds every individual accountable for his or her performance.

Although Carlson and others who have reached great heights of success have conscientiously set goals for themselves their entire lives, it is never too late to start. It is a rare gift to know exactly what you want from life at an early age, spend your early years preparing for it, and then go on to achieve incredible success in your chosen field. Most of us fol-

---

[1] Edwin McDowell, "Mellowed by Age, but Still a Tough Boss," *New York Times*, Sunday, 5 April 1992, Sec 3, 1; sec 3, 5.

low a much more erratic path and select a career based more on trial and error than on a master plan of some sort.

Build Flexibility into Plans

Plans should be flexible enough to respond quickly to unexpected events, and even when things go according to plan, our goals change as we grow and develop. Even the most motivated, best planners among us may find halfway through our careers that the business or profession has lost its luster and nothing we can do will change it. That's why a dentist may sell his practice to buy a horse ranch and a rising star in an investment banking firm quits to open a bed-and-breakfast in Vermont. In middle age, they found that they couldn't live with the career decisions they made years earlier.

It is remarkable, in fact, that any one of us has the wisdom or good luck to choose the right career when we are called upon to do so—as we approach high school graduation. Much of the college experience is aimed at helping us identify our strengths and weaknesses so that we can ultimately specialize in one area in which we have the greatest interest, aptitude, and ability.

If you opt to go to work rather than to college, the process is essentially the same. Most of us have a succession of jobs before we finally land in the right company or the right business that permits us to make the greatest contribution and reap the commensurate rewards. It is a process of elimination.

Learning from Trial and Error

We learn from trial and error what we do well and what we don't do so well; in fact, the lessons of failure are often far more vividly etched in memory than our successes. We don't often repeat spectacular mistakes. Instead, we file away the experience, and after the embarrassment and humiliation have passed, we are stronger, better educated and more likely to succeed the next time. Each experience—good and bad—is part of the process of shaping the person we wish to become and the ultimate career we desire for ourselves.

"Look Around" Objectives

Dwight Foster, head of Foster Partners, a New York–based Executive Search firm that places high-powered executives in senior corporate positions, says that many people fail because they fail to plan correctly or they overplan their lives. When I spoke with him recently by phone, he said: "They make certain assumptions—especially achievers—and they measure themselves against their peers. They have 'look around' objectives. They try to figure out what they need to do to lead the pack. When something goes wrong and they fall behind, they experience disconnectivity and they drift," he says.

In a fast-paced world where things always go wrong, where the path to the top is strewn with the corpses of those who for one reason or another were outflanked or overtaken by competitors, the ability to deal with adversity is critical to success. "These days," Foster says, "there is no long-term organizational loyalty. At one time, managers would agonize over the right thing to do, but that attitude is no longer pervasive in our society. Now it's: 'Harry just isn't cutting it any longer. He has to go.'"

Foster believes that a good test of the mettle of an executive is whether he has the sense to pick himself up and deal with changes in surroundings or in companies. If he is fired or otherwise deflected from his goal by forces beyond his control, does he have the ability to refocus his career? If not, the chances are good that he will drift from job to job and his background will become so fragmented that he will not have the qualifications for the position he desires.

Dealing with Adversity

Those who deal with setbacks most effectively are those who have a firm foundation: good family relationships and a strong network of friends and business associates. "The people who seem to survive adversity and maintain a high level of achievement are those who have sound spousal relationships," Foster says. "In many cases I have seen over a number of years, when an achiever is on his way up, he dumps his wife in favor of a younger woman who in turn dumps him when he is in a down cycle. I've seen it happen again and again.

"Well-rounded executives make time for their families and keep their marriages strong. One guy I know, the chief financial officer of a major corporation told me, 'I expect to spend my career here.' He was doing well and perfectly satisfied. Then a management succession issue arose. The head of a division with whom he had some disputes became the Chief Operating Officer and decided to choose his own CFO. The guy had done well, he had impeccable credentials, and now he was out of a job. But he had strong family support to carry him through the tough times, and he ended up with a better job at a better company."

Career Building in Stages

Foster believes a successful career is built in stages, with each position carefully chosen to meet our needs as we grow and develop. In the beginning, one should choose an "academy kind of company" that has an infrastructure that supports learning. Examples are large accounting firms and government agencies such as the FBI, the Environmental Protection Agency, or the Internal Revenue Service. Spend two or three years there and zero in on the areas in which you are most effective.

Second, secure a position with a growth organization, one that presents opportunities for additional growth, experience, and relationship building. It is important at this point to make sure that you share the organization's values. Growth companies tend to place great demands on their people and you will be required to make many sacrifices to get ahead. Spend five to eight years there, then determine what you are best suited to be.

No longer is there a stigma attached to multiple job changes, Foster says. "Back in the old days—the 1960s—the rule was that you should only make about three changes before you were thirty-five years old. With today's mobile work force and portable pension plans, it isn't uncommon to see people who have had five to seven—even ten—affiliations before they were thirty to thirty-five."

Choosing a Career at Eight Years of Age

Dave Thomas, the founder of Wendy's Old Fashioned Hamburgers, says he knew from the time he was eight years old that he wanted to be in the hamburger business, but he cooked a lot of chicken and fish and chips before he founded the highly successful hamburger chain he heads up today.

R. David Thomas was born July 2, 1932, in Atlantic City, New Jersey, and never knew his parents. He was adopted by a couple from Kalamazoo, Michigan, when he was six weeks old, but his adoptive mother died when he was five. He moved from state to state as his adoptive father sought work.

He was fired from his first job as a grocery delivery boy in Knoxville, Tennessee, at age twelve in a dispute over the length of a vacation. He got another job working at the soda counter in the local Walgreen's drugstore by lying about his age, but was fired again when his boss discovered Thomas wasn't sixteen years old. A stint at the lunch counter at Regas Restaurant followed where he worked hard during his twelve hour shifts, fearing that he would lose yet another job.

"I had lost two jobs already," he recalls, "and my father said he probably would have to support me for the rest of my life. He may have been joking, but it made an impression on me." He credits those early challenges with instilling in him a desire to succeed that led him to the top of his field. "Some people see my early life as an adversity, but it created a drive in me," he says. "I liked to make money, but money wasn't the only important thing. It was also the sense of accomplishment."

On His Own at Fifteen

When Thomas was fifteen, his family moved to Fort Wayne, Indiana, and he got a job as a busboy at the Hobby House Restaurant. When his family decided to move again, Thomas decided to stay. He took a room at the YMCA and, exhausted from working long hours at the restaurant, dropped out of school after completing the tenth grade.

He joined the U.S. Army when he turned eighteen and attended the army's cook and baker school before serving a tour of duty in Frankfurt, Germany, where he became one of the youngest soldiers ever to manage an enlisted men's club. When he was discharged, he returned to the Hobby House as a short-order cook, where he met his future wife, Lorraine, a waitress, whom he married in 1954.

Dave's Big Break

Thomas's big break came in the early 1960s when he met Colonel Harland Sanders. At the time he was working in a barbecue restaurant that he'd helped his boss, Hobby House owner Phil Clauss, open; the Colonel was touring the country promoting his Kentucky Fried Chicken franchise. Thomas's boss bought the franchise, and Thomas learned the chicken business.

In 1962, when Clauss acquired four failing KFC take-out stores in Columbus, Ohio, he offered Thomas a deal. If Thomas could turn the stores around, pay off a $200,000 deficit and make a profit, Clauss would give him forty-five percent of the Columbus franchise. "The Colonel told me not to come over here," Thomas said. "The stores were practically bankrupt; I had four kids and a wife, and I was making $135 a week. But I made up my mind that I was going to be in business for myself."

Thomas assessed the situation and from his years of experience in the restaurant business quickly realized that the principal reason the stores were failing was that they were offering too many items. He cut the menu from more than one hundred choices to a handful, mostly chicken and salads. He couldn't afford advertising, but to build awareness, he traded buckets of chicken for radio spots. Against the odds, the business prospered, and Thomas became a millionaire at age thirty-five when he sold the restaurants back to KFC for $1.5 million.

He continued with the chain, and worked his way up to regional operations director in charge of three hundred restaurants. He often traveled with Colonel Sanders, whom Thomas says he admired greatly, patterning his own management style after the kindly Sanders. "The Colonel was a pro," Thomas recalls fondly. "He used to say: be direct with people, tell 'em off when needed, but leave them feeling good."

After he left KFC, Thomas helped found Arthur Treacher's Fish & Chips, but he never lost interest in the hamburger business. In an industry that many experts considered already over-crowded with giant franchises such as McDonald's and Burger King, he launched yet another variety of the ubiquitous hamburger.

Founding Wendy's

The first Wendy's opened on November 15, 1969, at 257 East Broad Street in downtown Columbus. He named the restaurant after his then eight-year-old daughter, Melinda Lou, dubbed ''Wendy'' by her brother and sisters. The menu offered fresh, made-to-order hamburgers, chili, french fries, soft drinks, and a Frosty dairy dessert. Thomas's ambitions were modest. He hoped someday to have several restaurants around Columbus that would provide a place for his children to work in the summer.

Today, the former busboy and high school dropout presides over an empire that includes more than thirty-eight hundred restaurants throughout the U.S. and in thirty countries and territories around the world. Some 600 people work in Wendy's headquarters in Dublin, Ohio, and 130,000 people are employed by Wendy's and its franchises worldwide.

Because of his easygoing, down-home style and pervasive presence in Wendy's advertising, Thomas is one of the country's most popular television pitchmen. The company reported that by the end of 1991 the Dave Thomas campaign had generated a level of public awareness that surpassed the phenomenally successful ''Where's the Beef?'' campaign of the mid-1980s.

Thomas, who was himself put up for adoption as an infant, serves, by special invitation of the president of the United States, as the national spokesman for a special initiative on adoption. He supports a number of charities and, although he never finished high school himself, quickly points out to young people today that it is advisable to get as much education as possible.

Recipe for Success

In biographical materials distributed by Wendy's, Thomas capsulizes his recipe for success: ''I may not have a formal education,'' he says, ''but I was lucky enough to get a fantastic education from others about financing, motivating people, and building a business. You can't have a career until you get a job, and too many people want to start at the top. Just work hard and apply yourself. My recipe for success is hard work, patience, honesty, and total commitment.''

Key Points and Action Items

1. Goal setting is an essential element of success. Those who have specific, measurable goals always achieve more than those who do not.

2. Goals should be realistic and specific. Break them down into short-, intermediate-, and long-term objectives. Set a timetable for achieving your goals; go public with your plan. Monitor your progress and be persistent.

3. Build good family relationships and a strong network of friends and business associates. They are the greatest source of strength when you face adversity in your career.

4. Experts recommend building your career in stages. Start with an "academy" company that supports learning. Move to a growth organization, spend a few years there, then decide what you want to do in the longer term.

5. Commit yourself to achieving your goals and do the difficult things that are necessary to reach them. Pay attention to details. Big successes are built by paying attention to the little things others ignore.

10

The Importance of
Role Models

*People seldom improve when they have no
other model but themselves to copy after.*

—OLIVER GOLDSMITH

In his office overlooking downtown Pittsburgh, former Steelers superstar Lynn Swann displays photographs of the people he admires most. On one wall is a photo of the Silver Anniversary Super Bowl team, of which he is a member; another is a team photo of the pennant-winning Pittsburgh Pirates. But the photos that occupy the most prominent positions in his office are not those of other sports greats. They are pictures of his family and of General Colin Powell, chairman of the Joint Chiefs of Staff.

The placement of the photos is a reflection of his own values. Swann is justifiably proud of his sports achievements. He was a star player at the University of Southern California and during his years at the Steelers he played on four Super Bowl winning teams. He was selected as an NFL All Pro player, the most valuable player of the 1976 Super Bowl, NFL Man of the Year in 1981, and during his college career at USC he was chosen for the AP, UPI, and Kodak All America teams.

He has scores of awards commemorating his achievements in football.

Living in the Present

Unlike many other retired athletes, however, Swann doesn't spend his time reveling in past glories and replaying his moments in the sun. He lives very much in the present. Today, he's an ABC sports commentator, a reporter and occasional host on the network's Home Show, a product spokesman (for only those things he uses himself), and has appeared in dramatic and comedy roles on several popular television programs. He is also a frequent speaker at conventions and business meetings, and maintains a travel schedule that often requires him to be rehearsed and on camera early in the morning following a long, late-night flight and a few hours sleep.

It would be difficult—if not impossible—not to like Lynn Swann. His background is so rich and varied (he's cooked with Wolfgang Puck, founder of L.A.'s famous Spago restaurant, tap-danced with Gene Kelly, danced a modern ballet with Twyla Tharp and Peter Martins, and told stories with Mr. Rogers, among other things) that in a two-minute conversation he can find something in common with just about anyone. His face is recognized from coast to coast and in any restaurant in the country he can seldom eat a meal without a few fans asking for an autograph. Somehow, he seems to find time for them all, and he is unfailingly polite and friendly. He genuinely likes people, and they respond in kind.

I met Swann when we were discussing the possibility of his working with Masco Corporation to help promote the company's building products and home furnishings at trade shows and in product videos. He constantly amazed me with his ability somehow to find time to stay in touch, phoning from all over the country during breaks in college football games or between media interviews, and arranging to meet for lunch or dinner on one of his rare days off.

Giving Something Back

By any measure Swann has done well. He has earned a substantial income for most of his adult life, he has a spectacular home in an exclusive Pittsburgh suburb, expensive cars, countless friends, and a beautiful wife. When I asked him why he continues to drive himself so hard when he has already achieved more than most dream about, he didn't stop to think about his response. "It gives me a chance to help others," he said.

Swann's favorite cause is Big Brothers and Big Sisters of America, an organization for which he has served as national spokesman for more than a decade. He serves on the board of directors and helps with fund-raisers and speaks to groups all over the country on behalf of the organization, encouraging people to get involved. He is particularly interested in the plight of inner-city kids and devotes much of his scant free time to helping them. Most important, he shows by living example what it is possible to achieve when ability is backed up with rigorous training, determination, and perseverance. He is an exceptional role model for young people, who all too often have few positive examples to emulate.

Role Models for an Industry

In the business world, two college dropouts, Steve Wozniak and Steve Jobs, spawned entire new industries with the launch of their personal computer, and their example inspired countless other entrepreneurs to join the technological revolution. Silicon Valley in California (so called because of the electronics laboratories and semiconductor manufacturers located there) is filled with millionaires who patterned themselves after the early pioneers.

Electronics nuts who took great delight in tinkering with computers and telephone equipment, Jobs and Wozniak met through a mutual friend. When Jobs was still a teenager, he persuaded Wozniak to go into business with him selling "blue boxes," electronics units that mimicked the tones that ran telephone company switching systems and gave them free access to long distance service. They went door-to-door in the dorms at the University of California at Berkeley selling the units to students.

Wozniak was one of the thirty-two people who attended the first meeting of the Homebrew Computer Club that met in the Stanford Linear Accelerator Center, a modern complex in the hills above the university campus, in Palo Alto, California.

Widely regarded as the catalyst for the development of the electronics industry, Stanford University had already launched many electronics entrepreneurs.

A Stanford Tradition

Its first success occurred in 1909 when the school's president put up the money to market the wireless telephone invented by a local teenager. Stanford University graduates invented the loudspeaker and discovered that a vacuum tube could be used to amplify sound. When Bill Hewlett and David Packard formed a company to market an oscillator that Hewlett had invented, their professor, Fred Terman, who later was named dean of engineering at the school, lent money and encouragement to the project.

It was Terman's idea to build an industrial park on Stanford property that had been left to the university by its namesake, Leland Stanford, with the proviso that it could not be sold. By leasing the industrial park facilities to budding technology companies, the school could keep the land and comply with the terms of Stanford's will, and still raise the money to become a first-class research university. It was a good deal for everyone, and it established the model that others would follow.

In 1976, Wozniak, twenty-six, worked at Hewlett-Packard and his friend, Jobs, twenty-one, was at Atari. Wozniak often hung out with Jobs at Atari, occasionally moonlighting on a project so he could play the video games for free. In March of that year, they finished work on a preassembled computer circuit board that had no keyboard, case, sound, or graphics. They called it the Apple I.[1]

Investing Everything in the New Business

Soon afterward, Jobs sold his Volkswagen van and Wozniak sold his Hewlett-Packard programmable calculator to raise capital for their new business. The sale of the two most valuable items they owned generated $1,350 in cash, which they used to finance production of the programmable boards. Jobs leveraged an order from the Byte Shop, a local computer store,

---

[1]Apple is a registered trademark of Apple Computer, Inc.

for fifty Apple I boards to get credit in order to build the machines. They assembled them in his parents' garage. In July 1976, the Apple I board was released for sale to hobbyists and electronics enthusiasts at a price of $666.66.

Although historical accounts differ as to exactly what happened next, Apple says that in August, just five months after completion of the first programmable board, Jobs sought advice from legendary Atari founder Nolan Bushnell. Bushnell had helped launch the computer game industry when he founded Atari back in 1972 and became a Silicon Valley legend and a role model for aspiring entrepreneurs when he sold his company for a fortune to Warner Communications. Bushnell introduced Jobs to venture capitalist Don Valentine. In turn, Valentine referred him to Mike Markkula, the former manager of marketing for Intel Corporation and Fairchild Semiconductor.

Accustomed to the disciplines of marketing and the vagaries of business, Markkula recommended to Jobs and Wozniak that they develop a formal business plan. An effective plan has since become an entrenched custom among high-tech companies seeking investors, and usually includes a description of the product, including any unique or proprietary attributes, financial projections, and background information about the principal owners of the business.

The following January, Apple Computer was formally incorporated by Jobs, Wozniak, and their new partner and chairman, Mike Markkula. In addition to planning the fledgling company's marketing strategy, Markkula invested $250,000 in the business. His interest in the company later prompted other venture capitalists to invest in the tiny business.

Launching a Revolution

In their first business plan, Jobs and Wozniak set a goal to reach $500 million in sales in ten years, a mark they would pass in half the time. The personal computer that they developed revolutionized the business and the company they founded with $1,350 became synonymous with technological change.

Like most companies, Apple has been through many ups and downs since then, but its mission still reflects many of the values of its founders. In its literature the company profiles itself this way: "Apple Computer, Inc., develops, manufactures and markets personal computer systems for use in business, education, science, engineering and government. A recognized pioneer and innovator in the personal computer industry, Apple does business in more than 120 countries. Apple has redefined computing to mean empowerment of the individual. It seeks through technology to provide people with easy and affordable access to information and computing power."

The business that two intense young entrepreneurs began in a garage fifteen years earlier, in 1991 employed over fourteen thousand people and reported sales of more than $6.3 billion and net income of over $309 million. In 1991, sales of Macintosh computers increased more than sixty percent, according to the company, making it the fastest-growing major computer brand in the U.S., Europe, and the Pacific region. That year the company again startled the world when it forged an alliance with arch-rival International Business Machines and with Motorola, Inc. to develop advanced microprocessor technology that will be used in new Macintosh and IBM systems.[2]

In the years that followed Apple's founding, academics, entrepreneurs, venture capitalists, and those who wished to do business with them studied Jobs and Wozniak's methodology, hoping to replicate their success. Stanford University graduated thousands of fast-track engineers who were promptly snapped up by technology-based companies in the surrounding area. In turn, they got a few years of experience, then quit to form their own ventures, seduced by the successes of those who had gone before them.

Win Some, Lose Some

Nolan Bushnell became a cult figure in the technological revolution despite a spectacular failure in the mid-1980s with Pizza Time Theater, Inc., a chain of pizza/video parlors. In

[2]Apple Computer, Inc. and Frank Rose, *West of Eden: The End of Innocence at Apple Computer* (New York: Viking Penguin, 1989) 19–35.

1990, he launched a new venture, a multimedia system that can be attached to any television or stereo.

According to *Forbes* magazine, "Bushnell, who has founded some twenty companies over the years, makes no apologies for his hit-and-miss record. 'I play the game quite differently from other venture capitalists,' he says, 'in that I am very, very happy to fund a company very thinly to test it, and if it does not look extremely promising, I am more than happy to let it flounder. I am looking for big successes.' "[3]

Bushnell, Jobs, and others invested in promising new technologies, inspiring countless budding entrepreneurs to reach for the brass ring. Many succeeded, adding to the lore of the industry and the explosive growth of technology-based businesses. High-tech communities replete with their own research universities, venture capitalists, and entrepreneurs sprang up along Boston's Route 128, in the "Research Triangle" near Raleigh, North Carolina, in Austin near the University of Texas, and along the East–West Tollway in suburban Chicago.

State governments, anxious to attract start-up companies, formed "incubators," patterned after the Stanford University industrial park. They offered low-rent space with phone, secretarial, and other services to meet the needs of emerging high-tech companies during their difficult start-up time. Clubs and societies were formed and meetings arranged and seminars given (keynoted by successful high-tech entrepreneurs who told the story of their own achievements) to allow would-be inventors to present their business plans to venture capitalists hoping to discover the next Apple Computer.

Cloning the Process

In the early 1980s, when he was named partner-in-charge of the high-technology practice in the Chicago business unit of the Big Six accounting firm of KPMG Peat Marwick, Michael Lavin cast about for a big idea to launch the practice. With characteristic intensity he studied the field, attempting to identify the characteristics necessary to succeed in an industry that was still in the early stages of development. He concluded

---

[3]Reed Aberlson, "Bushnell is Back," *Forbes* (August 20, 1990), 109.

that most of the elements were in place except role models. Chicago had plenty of venture capitalists, attorneys, inventors, consultants, and the like, and there was an informal network to share information about opportunities and successes.

Lavin headed up a team whose mission was to develop a plan to recognize and publicize success stories, to provide role models for Chicago's high-technology industry during its formative years. Peat Marwick would sponsor the program to help establish the firm and Lavin as leaders in the emerging industry. The team included Richard Rotman and his account team at the public relations firm of Ruder, Finn & Rotman (now Ruder & Finn), and me.

As we considered and eliminated the alternatives, we finally opted to sponsor an annual awards program, called High Tech Entrepreneur of the Year, to identify and recognize those who had introduced a commercially successful high-technology product. Anyone could be nominated; judging would be conducted by an independent blue-ribbon panel composed of leaders in the industry. Winners would be recognized at an awards luncheon; each would receive a limited-edition sculpture designed by Chicago artist Zelda Werner especially for the competition.

A competition, of course, is not exactly a novel idea, but it was one that had not been done in the high-tech industry. If we executed it well, we firmly believed it would succeed in meeting our objective to identify role models that others could learn from and emulate.

To ensure that we could properly publicize the event to attract entrants, we formed an alliance with the Illinois Institute of Technology and *Crain's Chicago Business*. IIT would help identify those who were successfully commercializing new technologies and *Crain's* would publicize the competition to the business community. We also worked with the state chamber of commerce and its affiliate members in cities and towns throughout the state to distribute information packets and nomination forms.

The competition was the right idea at the right time. The first year there were scores of qualified entrants, the awards banquet was sold out, and the governor of Illinois delivered the keynote address. Resulting publicity for the winners helped their businesses grow; it established Lavin and Peat Marwick as leaders in Chicago's high-tech community, and it accelerated the development of start-up companies. Beginning entrepreneurs learned from those who had already succeeded about the intricacies of organizing the business, attracting investment, marketing the product, and managing the growth of the company. The competition helped bring together numerous inventors and investors and to establish alliances that resulted in numerous new business ventures.

Building upon Success

The program was so successful from its inception that S. Thomas Moser, then national director of Peat's high-technology practice, encouraged others to adopt the idea and sponsor similar competitions in their market areas. The High Tech Entrepreneur of the Year competition went on to become an institution in the firm. Similar events were sponsored by several other offices in the U.S. and in other countries. It was a powerful example of the influence positive role models can exert.

The lesson in this example is that success in any endeavor has definite principles that can be learned. Role models provide shortcuts that allow us to avoid costly, time-consuming mistakes and focus our attention on proven techniques.

Choosing Role Models

One achiever who makes mentoring and role modeling an integral part of her success philosophy is my friend and business associate Paula Blanchard, the former First Lady of Michigan. When she realized that her life was being consumed by her husband's ambitions, Blanchard decided to take control of her life. She got a divorce, moved out of the Governor's Residence, finished the course work for a master's degree at Michigan State University, and started her own audio/video production company.

She credits her role models with giving her the courage to strike out on her own and the determination to reach the goals she regularly sets for herself. Her maternal grandmother was a primary influence in her life. Widowed at a young age with three children under age six, she began teaching school to support her family. She never remarried, returned to college to comply with more stringent educational requirements, and traveled the world. It was from her grandmother's example that Blanchard learned that it is possible to live a rich life alone.

Her parents also served as role models, and her hobby of building and refinishing furniture began when as a youngster she helped her father with household projects. In an interview in her Southfield, Michigan, office, she recalled, "I thought what he was doing in the basement was so much more interesting than what my mother was doing in the kitchen. He was always fixing things, building furniture, painting and wallpapering, and teaching himself new hobbies and skills.

"He encouraged me to do the same. He encouraged my curiosity, he encouraged me to try new things, and he rewarded me with praise when I succeeded. When I failed, he taught me what I needed to know so I wouldn't fail again. He taught me that I could do anything I set my mind to if I was disciplined enough, committed enough, and learned enough," Blanchard says.

Today, Blanchard is a vice president of Casey Communications Management, Inc., a leading midwestern public relations and public affairs counseling firm affiliated with Shandwick, plc. Michigan State University's College of Education has given her its Distinguished Alumnae Award, and she holds honorary doctorate degrees from three universities. In addition to her other responsibilities, Blanchard writes a monthly column for *Detroit Metropolitan Woman* and is a frequent speaker on women's issues and other topics.

Study the Lives of Others

Blanchard advises that it isn't always necessary to know your role models to learn from them. A voracious reader herself, she suggests reading self-help books, biographies, and autobiographies to learn about how others faced the challenges in their lives. She was inspired by the life of Marjorie Rawlings, who she describes as a "shirttail relative" on her father's side of the family.

Rawlings gave up a life of leisure, divorced her very successful husband, picked up stakes, moved to Florida, bought an orange grove, and converted her front porch to a writing studio. She went on to become a Pulitzer Prize-winning writer. Her influence upon Blanchard was primarily through her books.

Take an Active Role

For more direct interaction with role models, Blanchard suggests taking an active role. "Don't wait for them to invite you to work with them and learn from them," she says. If she respects and admires someone, she doesn't hesitate to tell them so and ask them to be her mentor. She refuses to be one of those people who wait for someone to chose them, to identify them as someone they would like to mentor.

"Most people are flattered when you say, 'I like the way you operate or I really respect what you've accomplished in your career, and I would like to learn from you," she says. She says she's asked both men and women, and the experience has been very enlightening and rewarding in her professional development. "You can't sit around and wait to be asked," she notes. "It goes with taking control of your life, taking charge, taking responsibility for your own happiness and your own development. No one will do it for you. You have to do it for yourself."

Maintain Objectivity

Role models should not be confused with infatuation or hero worship. To learn effectively from those who have been successful or those whose personal characteristics we admire requires considerable objectivity. We must rate them not on a scale of likability, but on a selective basis that allows us to identify the attributes we would like to emulate and the specific techniques they employ to achieve a desired result.

We should not attempt to become a copy of the person from whom we wish to learn. Any personal characteristics we wish to adopt or techniques we would like to learn to apply should fit with our own personalities and value systems. Shy, introspective people, for example, may be drawn to opposites—those who are gregarious and outgoing—and vice versa. They may become great friends because their personalities complement each other (one likes to talk, the other lets him), but it is highly unlikely that they will ever be alike. They may learn from each other how to strengthen the areas in which they are weak, but mimicking another in every detail quickly labels one as a phony.

For example, most of us understand and comply with laws and regulations. We don't steal and we don't violate company policy, for obvious reasons. In addition to the public disgrace that is likely to accompany such behavior, there is a very practical economic reason. If we break the law or are fired for violations of company policy, we greatly diminish our lifetime earning power. The end result would be to sacrifice a promising career for a temporary gain. Any way you view it, it is a poor trade.

Shades of Gray

Within the limits of the law, policy, and regulations, however, there are many shades of gray. Some are acceptable to us in the context of our personal value systems and religious and moral leanings, and some are not. For instance, many business arrangements are handshake agreements based upon a verbal understanding between two people. Some individuals have no qualms about violating the agreement if they later change their minds, or if it turns out that there was an honest misunderstanding about the responsibilities of each in the deal.

Such agreements are difficult to enforce because it usually comes down to one person's word against another. Yet, there are many whose promise is as good as a contract drawn up by the best lawyers in the world, people who will live up to the promise they made regardless of the personal sacrifice required—simply because they gave their word. The latter is obviously a better role model, but it is still possible to learn something from the former without adopting personal traits of which you disapprove.

Accentuate the Positive; Overlook the Negative

To emulate the positive behavior of others while overlooking the negative is not easy. We are all impressionable and we are influenced—for better or worse—by others more than we sometimes like to admit.

Jason Livingston grew up with his mother in a small house in London's south end dreaming of being a sprinter like the famous Canadian Ben Johnson. He decorated his room with posters of Johnson, and he studied Johnson's races to learn everything he could about the great sprinter.

When Livingston began to run competitively himself, he mimicked Johnson's style, particularly his explosive start off the blocks. He even shaved his head just like his hero, and much to his delight fellow athletes began to call him "Baby Ben." As he worked and trained, Livingston became better and better, eventually winning the sixty-meter European Indoor Championships. British track and field experts labeled him a "bright young star."

In 1988, when Johnson was stripped of his title after it was discovered that he had illegally used steroids, Livingston was devastated. He told reporters: "It was like part of me died. I could not live with myself being an Olympic champion knowing that I cheated. It is a shame people have to go to such lengths."

When he was twenty-one, Livingston's dream came true. His years of devotion and training paid off when he qualified for the 1992 British Olympic team in the one hundred-meter dash. On July 28, 1992, he arrived in Barcelona full of hope and dreams. The next day, he was sent home in disgrace, suspended for life from the Olympics by British authorities. He had failed his drug test. Like his idol, he had succumbed to the temptation of steroids.

A Real Hero

Sports columnist Mitch Albom points to British runner Marcus Adam as a real hero of the 1992 Olympics and a far better role model. In one of the earlier one hundred-meter heats, Adam got off to a bad start, but recovered, and almost caught up by the time the leaders reached the finish line. The finish was so close that it took a few minutes for officials to determine who would make the grade. Only the top four would qualify for the semifinals.

When the results were official, Adam had finished in fifth place—by a hundredth of a second. "He was silent for a moment," Albom says. "Then he shrugged. 'Well, my start was rubbish. I was hoping I could make up for it, but I couldn't.

No worries. I'm in one piece and I'm still alive, so everything's OK.'

"And then he smiled.

"I have never seen an athlete—especially under those conditions—take defeat with such grace," the columnist says. "And I wish this Livingston kid could have seen it. I wish he had chosen his countryman to be his hero, instead of Ben Johnson."[4]

[4]Mitch Albom, "The Lesson Should Be Simple: Don't Be Like Ben," *Detroit Free Press*, 1 August 1992, 1B, 5B.

Key Points and Action Items

1. Choose people of character to emulate. Select those who give something back to their community or their profession—people who go out of their way to help others. Kindness and generosity are traits exhibited by people with good character.

2. Every industry has leaders. Learn about those in your business or profession and get to know them, if possible. Identify what they do well and learn from their successes.

3. Don't confuse role models with hero worship or select role models simply because they are likable. Instead, identify the attributes that you would like to emulate and the techniques they used to achieve a desired result.

4. It is not always necessary to be personally acquainted with role models. Study the lives of successful people and learn from their experience how they overcame adversity and capitalized on opportunity.

5. Take an active role in selecting role models and mentors. Don't wait to be asked. If you like the way certain individuals operate and believe you could learn from them, tell them so. Ask them to help you, but make sure you give something of value to them in return.

11

A Winning Personality

The secret of managing is to keep the guys who hate you away from the guys who are undecided.

—CASEY STENGEL

More than twenty years ago when I got my first corporate communications job at a manufacturing company based in suburban Chicago, I received a call from the office receptionist telling me that there was a salesman in the lobby who would like to speak to the person who buys commercial printing. She asked if I would be willing to talk to him.

Having spent the previous several years selling insurance and advertising to put myself through college, I knew well the courage required to make cold calls. I had some time, and I agreed to spend a few minutes with this guy who was going door-to-door in office complexes introducing himself and his company.

His name was Wayne Bilut, he said, and he was a printing salesman. He'd just started with the company and had not yet developed a clientele, so he was spending his free time making calls in the hope that he would find a few customers who would give him a chance to prove himself. "We offer highest quality printing at competitive prices," he said, "and I will personally make sure that our quality work is delivered to you when you expect it at the price we quoted to you.'' He went on to say that if we gave him an order, there would never be any unpleasant surprises. He would keep us informed about the job, and he would handle the problems. We would get the best service it was possible to deliver.

It happened that I had a small job that I was working on that had not yet been assigned to one of our regular printers, so I gave Bilut the specifications and asked for a price quote. He responded quickly and I gave him the job. He delivered everything exactly as promised, and gradually I gave him bigger and bigger orders until he became the company's primary supplier of printing.

Top Salesman

Bilut went on to become one of the top printing salesmen in America. At his peak, he personally sold between eight and one-half and ten million dollars worth of printing a year for three consecutive years, more than the total volume of many commercial printers. In the more than two decades I've known Bilut, I've changed companies and locations, and sometimes I have been a customer and sometimes not for various reasons, but he has always stayed in touch. I've introduced him to friends and business associates, and I've never hesitated to give him an unqualified recommendation, something I do not do easily.

I value my friends and business associates, and I have high expectations—for myself and for the people with whom I work. I would never recommend anyone unless I have complete confidence in them. To do so would be a disservice both to my friends and associates and to the person I recommend. Neither would be pleased with the outcome and both would hold me responsible. Bilut has always met or exceeded my highest expectations. If he says he will do something, you can count on it. He has never failed to deliver on a commitment.

"Pacing" Technique

Bilut has another quality that I regularly find amazing. It is what Donald J. Moine and John H. Herd refer to as ''pacing'' in their book *Modern Persuasion Strategies: The Hidden Advantage in Selling*. What they mean by pacing is to reveal your personality traits that are similar to those exhibited by your prospect. They define pacing as "a sophisticated form of matching or mirroring key aspects of another's behavioral preference.

"You are pacing," according to the authors, "when the prospect gets the feeling that you and he (or she) think alike and look at problems in similar ways. When this happens, the prospect identifies with you and finds it easy and natural to agree with you. You seem like emotional twins. Pacing works, because like attracts like."[1]

Moine and Herd traveled around the country talking to the top salespeople and watching them work. They concluded that some people instinctively "paced" with prospects while others had to work at it, but that the end results were the same. Salespeople proficient at pacing outperformed others by huge margins.

We Buy from Those We Like

After many years of working with both buyers and sellers of products and services—individually and in groups—I am convinced that people will always find a way to do business with people they like. Regardless of the sophistication of the purchasing procedure or the expense of the product or service, we all have a natural tendency to do business with people with whom we are comfortable. We make the decision emotionally, then work out the logical basis of the decision later, assuming, of course, that price, quality, and service between competitors are relatively constant.

Bilut says salespeople often forget the old axiom in business that a deal is not a good deal unless it is a good deal for everyone involved. Every person should benefit from the transaction. When I asked him to identify the characteristics that lead to successful sales careers, he said: "Salesmen sometimes forget the importance of this idea in building relationships. They always say 'gimme'—gimme an order or gimme

---

[1]Phillip M. Albert, "Something New in Selling," a review of *Modern Persuasion Strategies: The Hidden Advantage in Selling*, by Donald J. Moine and John H. Herd, *PMA Adviser* (January 1986), 3.

a commission, but they don't respond in kind. They overlook the importance of investing in your customers.

"People want to be thanked somehow. You have to take action to let them know you appreciate them. Talk is cheap. Everyone says 'thank you for the order.' Really successful people spend time with their clients and customers; they let them know they are important. Buyers are human, and they need to know that the people they are dealing with are human. They need something besides simply exchanging paperwork; they need to feel good about life in general. People interaction makes the difference in building long-term relationships. Only a shortsighted sales person tries to build a relationship on price alone."

I've never been able to tell for sure whether pacing comes naturally to Bilut or whether he has to work at it, but I suspect that it is some of both. He always finds something in common with his customers, regardless of their diversity, something he says is not easy and "cannot be done in a sales call. You have to get them away from the office—out to lunch or dinner or something—to find things in common. You need to understand their goals and career strategies so you can determine how to best help them and where you fit in." To get to know each other well enough to share that kind of personal information demands that you spend time together, Bilut believes.

First, Like Yourself

In his career as a top producing salesman and the manager of other fast-track salespeople, Bilut has come to the conclusion that before you are the kind of person other people like, you must first like yourself. Being successful means that you have to be good at your job and as a person, he says. It begins with self-confidence. "If you have confidence in yourself and you share information about yourself, people give information back about themselves.

"Sales people often have trouble one-on-one," he says. "They don't realize that selling involves far more work than just gaining product knowledge. They need to understand that they are going to be working with varied people with many different interests. To know and understand your customers, you must have a sincere interest in who they are. Make them feel important because they *are* important. They are your customers. Spend the time to get to know them.''

Most salespeople talk too much, Bilut believes. They should listen more. He advises those who have trouble relating to strangers to make a list of questions to ask that will help open up a conversation. Plan how you will ask questions about your prospect's personal life, the organization he works for and how he fits into it, about the individual and his goals. If you can't get personal with someone, you can't get the information you need to best help him or her.

"Make sure he understands the support principle, that you as a salesperson are in business to help your customer and that you have the confidence of your organization and its strength behind you," Bilut advises. "Your clients and customers need to know you are reliable. This becomes increasingly important the higher a person gets in his or her company. Your customers need to know that they are dealing with reliable people to whom projects can be turned over with the knowledge that they will be handled properly.

"Economics today dictate that every person must do more. If someone has ten projects going at the same time, he needs to know that you are effectively managing those for which you are responsible, that he doesn't have to worry about them because you are. You are checking its status, corresponding, and making phone calls required to keep the project on track. Staying in touch and regularly reporting on the project's status gives them the feeling that everything is okay.

Seek Other Achievers

"Achievers look for other achievers. They like working with people who plan ahead and pay attention to details," Bilut continues. "They like to know their person is there, that they take responsibility for the job. My customers don't have to call me; I call them and keep them updated and informed. If I'm out and can't call them personally, someone who works for me will call them. We never leave our customers in the dark.''

Bilut believes that such focus on the customer must permeate the organization, and it has to start at the top. "If you surround yourself with good people, trust them, and give them the freedom to operate,'' he says, ''they will make sure that your customers get the attention they need and deserve.''

This is not something that people do naturally. It has to be learned, nurtured, and developed over time. Most people are reluctant to share information, and salespeople are especially guarded, Bilut says, because they are afraid that if they say too much, someone will learn enough to steal the account. Rather than working as a team with the inside people, salespeople are secretive, and often don't provide sufficient information to allow others to do their jobs well.

Keep Others Informed

Bilut recommends the opposite approach. ''Talk to your people,'' he advises. ''Tell them about the customer and the politics at the customer's organization. Tell them who can be trusted, who to talk to and who to avoid. Make them part of the project. If you shut them out, they won't respond when you need their assistance.

''My people know they have the authority to make decisions and that I will support their decision. I won't second-guess them later, even in such sensitive areas as pricing and scheduling. Any member of the team can make a decision and we all support it. When people have that kind of authority and responsibility, it gives them a feeling that they are an important part of the business, that they have control of their lives and their jobs. To succeed in sales, you must have the support of your people. They make or break you.''

That attitude seems to characterize people who have achieved great success in any field. Problems begin to occur for us when we become so full of our own wonderfulness that we allow our egos to run away with us. As long as we recognize that we are in business to serve our customers, we maintain our perspective. When we forget about those who have made us what we are, they forget us and the effect on the business is disastrous.

In a world filled with rude people who seem to dislike their jobs, their companies, and their customers, it is easy to stand out from the crowd. Just being courteous and friendly to people is enough to make them stop and take notice. If you couple a pleasant demeanor with a quality product and good service, the results can be spectacular.

Total Customer Satisfaction

The automobile business has taken a lot of lumps in recent years for poor quality and service, but it is also a fertile ground for success stories. In an industry that struck a deal with the Better Business Bureau to arbitrate disputes between manufacturers, dealers, and customers, when a customer of Precision Toyota in Tucson, Arizona, contacts the BBB, he or she is asked: "Have you spoken to Jack Rowe?"

The owner of Precision Toyota, Rowe has a simple three-point program to ensure customer satisfaction:

1. The customer is never wrong.
2. If a car has a problem, we guarantee that we will fix it to the customer's satisfaction.
3. The customer will not be inconvenienced.

Several years ago in an interview, Rowe told us that in his years in business, he has found that what upsets customers most is a problem that doesn't get resolved. "There isn't anything that can't be repaired because there is nothing on the car that can't be replaced, but it is upsetting to a customer if the problem keeps recurring. When that happens, I personally take charge until the problem is corrected," he says.

"If an item has to be totally replaced, I offer the customer my personal car to use until the work is completed, whether it takes an hour, a day, or two days. It is a visible demonstration that we are doing everything we can to the best of our ability to solve their problem. I then get the service manager and a mechanic together, and we determine how to best correct the problem. We have never had a problem that we couldn't solve when we address it this way. Where there is a problem, there is a reason. All we have to do is find it."

A Replacement Automobile

If it is a problem that might affect the safety of the automobile (something that happens very infrequently, Rowe says) and the customer says it has happened more than once, Precision takes the car back. "If we've tried to repair the car twice, no matter what the reason, and we haven't corrected the problem, we tell them to come down and pick out a new car," he says. "They don't have to pay tax, license, or anything else. They just get a new car.

"It is something we've been doing for years because we do not want our customers to ever be in an unsafe car. After the car is repaired, we make it a company car and one of our managers drives it for three or four months to make absolutely certain that the problem is corrected and that the car is again completely safe.

"There is no magic to keeping your customers happy," Rowe says. "The only way to do it is to go the extra mile with them, to put yourself in their shoes. Many of us who have been in the automobile business for twenty-five or thirty years forget what the person who drives the car is really expecting. The customer is paying a lot of money for reliability, and that is exactly what he or she is expecting—even in a used car. They are buying transportation, and when it fails to be safe or reliable, the dealer has a problem and we have to face it. Dealers who don't like that idea are in the wrong business.

"We have a rule that we will not let the customer leave and not be satisfied and happy. Realistically, there are some situations in which you can't reach a satisfactory compromise, but they are very rare. Both we and Toyota want the customer to be completely satisfied, so we work together to make sure it happens. We make the decision on the spot, even if it is an unreasonable settlement that we know will cost us money. It makes no sense to spend $25,000 a month on advertising, then try to save $250 on goodwill. As the old cliché goes, that's penny wise and dollar foolish," Rowe says. It comes as no surprise that much of his sales volume is generated from repeat business.

Evergreen's Smith: A Living Example

Another who is totally dedicated to his customers is Delford M. ("Del" to all who know him) Smith, the chairman and founder of McMinnville, Oregon–based Evergreen International Aviation, Inc. I met him a few years ago when Mike Ritt, executive director of The Napoleon Hill Foundation, asked me to write a profile about Smith for a book the Foundation was publishing. Smith had been selected by the Foundation's board of directors as an individual who best exemplified and applied the success principles that Napoleon Hill wrote about.

Smith started Evergreen in 1960 with two helicopters that he bought with no money down. The only collateral he had was his track record as a helicopter pilot for a McMinnville flying service and a prodigious capacity for hard work. He proved his mettle flying transport missions and fire-fighting jobs for the forestry service in the Pacific Northwest, and ferried parts, supplies, and oil field workers on Alaska's North Slope and in the Middle East.

Uncompromising Quality

''Quality Without Compromise'' was the foundation upon which the organization was built, and it is the company's motto today. Smith had three axioms that continue to serve as Evergreen's guiding beacon:

1. Performance is the only thing that counts!
2. Looking after the customer properly is our reason for being.
3. What we do should be beneficial for mankind.

He and his crew take great pride in the services they have provided in support of this vision. Evergreen plucked country singer Hank Williams, Jr. from a Montana mountainside when he was injured in a fall, flew the Shah of Iran and the daughter of José Napoléon Duarte to safety when their lives were threatened, and the company stayed in Vietnam several days after the last U.S. military plane left to evacuate Royal Dutch Shell employees and their families.

Evergreen crews have fought fires around the world, river blindness in Africa, famine in Ethiopia, and helped search for oil in every oil patch in the free world. Smith himself received the Frederick L. Feinberg Award for his daring rescue of a young girl during a flood. Disregarding his own safety, Smith flew his helicopter at night in winds up to sixty miles per hour, searching until he found the girl trapped on a small island in the middle of a raging river. According to news accounts at the time, the island was within a foot of submersion when Smith lifted her to safety.

Smith's unswerving dedication to meeting his customers' needs and his tireless dedication to quality has fueled the growth of his privately owned aviation empire. In 1991, Evergreen posted revenues of $477 million and owned a fleet of aircraft valued at about $1 billion. Estimates placed his personal net worth at around $600 million.

The Importance of Physical Presence

At sixty-one years of age, Smith is as committed today as he was when he began the company more than thirty years ago. He is a great believer in physical presence for the company and all its employees. The chairman was on board the Evergreen Gulfstream II executive jet that was the first commercial airplane to land in Kuwait City after the shooting stopped in the war with Iraq.

He was already in the area because for months prior to the war Evergreen had ferried troops and supplies to the war zone. His philosophy of service is beautiful in its simplicity: "First, you have to sell yourself," he says. "Second, sell the need. Third, sell the solution and have it close at hand. We sell real solutions to real problems."

On the ground in Kuwait City, Smith quickly assessed the situation. The city was desperately short of medical supplies, drinking water, and electrical power. With characteristic decisiveness, he had the seats removed from his executive jet, and for the next several weeks Smith and his crew made four trips a day from pickup points in Saudi Arabia to Kuwait City, ferrying in bottled water, medicine, and generators.

It would be hard *not* to like Smith. He is a man who has his feet firmly on the ground and a clear view of what he is about and what he wishes to accomplish. Despite his feats of derring-do and his obvious success, he is a modest, unassuming, disarmingly polite gentleman who has three passions in life: sons Mike, twenty-five, an Air National Guard F-15 pilot,

Mark, twenty-four, a recent American Racing Series Rookie of the Year, and his Evergreen family.

He still lives in the home where he raised the boys. When I visited McMinnville to interview him, Smith invited me to stay at his home rather than at a hotel. He gave me a tour of the grounds, including a recreation center—complete with an indoor pool and game room—that the boys helped build as teenagers. I bunked in Mike's room amid his racing trophies, an appropriate prelude to an early morning Evergreen flight to Phoenix the next day to watch the younger Smith race in the Indy Light series.

Smith gives his people free rein and great responsibility at an early age. He supports and encourages them, makes them part of the family, and takes great pride in their achievements. In turn, they give him a tireless commitment to his vision of quality without compromise and unflagging loyalty.

What Others Say

In addition to his plain-spoken ways and down-to-earth manner, the thing that most impressed me about Smith was the things others said about him when he wasn't around. Instead of the perfunctory accolades about the boss that often characterize interviews with employees, Evergreen people told me personal stories about how he helps them, takes an interest in their families and careers, and how he anonymously helps others.

When a young African woman working as a waitress in a Washington, D.C., hotel told him she was saving to bring her family to America, he left $1,000 in an envelope with her name on it at the front desk. It was his contribution to help her reach her goal. When a McMinnville bank, on whose board of directors he served, got in trouble because some local borrowers were unable to repay their loans, Smith put up the cash to keep the bank afloat. "We are not going to let down our investors and the citizens who have money on deposit here," he said.

His people say that Smith is a tough taskmaster who demands excellence from everyone in the organization—but he never asks more from anyone else than he gives himself. He works as hard today as he did during the infancy of the company when he and his crew drove trucks most of the night hauling helicopters and support equipment to a customer's location, slept for a few hours, then got up at first light to fly a crop-dusting job.

Grounded in Character

Smith is a man whose winning personality is firmly grounded in his character. He is what he appears to be. Evergreen Holding Company president Joe Sharp sums up the boss this way: "Del is an absolute capitalist, but he truly believes that in the end we will all be measured by what we've given back, not by what we've taken. He's a man of action. He says, 'Let's get the job done and not worry about congratulations and frills. Our job is to take care of our customers and not spend too much time worrying about who gets the credit for a quality job. If the organization looks good, we all look good.' "

In today's mobile, fast-paced, high-tech, brief-encounter world, it is gratifying to find someone in a high position whose public persona and private character are identical. This is not always the case. Frequently, we are positively influenced by the power of someone's personality, only to discover later that his or her character is severely flawed. A few TV evangelists and politicians leap to mind as notorious examples of those whose strong personalities were built upon a weak foundation. Yet they sometimes manage to take advantage of millions of people before they are discovered.

More than Charm Required

We learn early in life that people respond when we turn on the old charm. When as children we compete for attention from authority figures such as parents and teachers, we do so on the basis of personality. When we apply for a job—particularly as beginners, when there are a large number of competitors with essentially the same qualifications—personality is often the only (if subtle) differentiating factor. As a result, some people assume that they can get along quite well their entire lives on the basis of a winning personality.

They never tire of selling others on the basis of their superficial personality traits, going from person to person, taking advantage of them. When one group or person becomes dissatisfied with the one-sided relationship, they move on to someone else. World-champion poker player Amarillo Slim once advised, "When you sit down at the table, look around for a sucker. If you don't see one, get out of there. The sucker is you!"

Like a successful business relationship, the best kind of a friendship is one in which everyone contributes and benefits equally. In a lifetime of moving around and meeting new people, I have discovered that when you begin a new job or move into a new neighborhood, the people who most want to be your friends are the ones you will likely discover later that you don't really want to be your friends. Often they are the ones who grab onto every person who comes along to use them to their own ends. People who are successful, happy, secure, and well adjusted are not looking for new friends. Whenever I've lost sight of that axiom, I've always regretted it.

Choose Friends Carefully

We are attracted to others because of their personalities, but we should decide on the basis of their character whether or not we wish to be close friends or merely business or social acquaintances. If a relationship always involves your giving or helping and not receiving equivalent emotional gratification in return, it is an unfair and unbalanced relationship that you will likely grow to resent. The chances are good that the person in question is using his or her personality to take advantage of you. Choose your friends carefully. Don't let them choose you.

Evaluate yourself as critically as you evaluate others. Make sure you measure up, that you are a person others respect and enjoy being around. A winning personality—one that will enable you to achieve sustained success—is one that reflects a person of strong character.

Key Points and Action Items

1. Learn to "pace" or align your personality traits that are similar to those of someone with whom you wish to do business. People always find a reason to do business with those they like.

2. Customer focus must permeate your organization. Surround yourself with good people, trust them, and give them the freedom to operate. They will make sure your customers get the attention they need and deserve.

3. Never leave a customer's problem unresolved. Go the extra mile with the customer. Put yourself in his shoes, and take whatever action is necessary to fix the problem.

4. Physical presence is important. Sell yourself first and the need second. Third, sell the solution and have it close at hand. Sell real solutions to real problems.

5. Make sure your winning personality is firmly grounded in good character. Make sure that you deserve the respect of others.

12

Using the Brain God Gave You

Only he who can see the invisible can do the impossible.

—FRANK L. GAINES

More than a half century ago, Swiss inventor Georges de Mestral decided to go for a walk in the woods with his dog. No doubt he enjoyed the peace and solitude in the cool dark woods. There he could let his mind wander; he could relax.

When he returned home, he discovered that lost in thought, he had apparently wandered through a patch of cockleburs. The dog's coat and his wool trousers were filled with them. As he tried to remove the burrs, instead of being annoyed, he was enthralled by the strength and holding power of the burrs. Fascinated, he placed one under a microscope to have a closer look. He discovered that the burrs had hundreds of tiny hooks that had become entangled in the nap of his trousers and in the dog's coat.

The Invention of Velcro[1]

De Mestral began to experiment, trying to duplicate the tiny hooks of the burrs and the loops of the woven fabric. He

---

[1]Velcro is a registered trademark of Velcro Fastening Systems, Velcro USA, Manchester, N.H.

believed that if he could perfect the process, he could create an efficient, lightweight fastener that could be used in a variety of commercial applications. He called his invention Velcro, a combination of the words velvet and crochet (French for hook).

The inventor perfected the hook and loop technique relatively quickly by simply duplicating the properties of the lowly cocklebur, but available materials limited the product's strength and durability. By sheer luck, a synthetic fiber called nylon was invented by Wallace H. Carothers of the Du Pont Chemical Company at about the same time. The strength of this tough artificial fiber gave de Mestral's invention the holding power it needed.

The problem was that nylon was too tough. The inventor couldn't find a machine that could cut the material into tiny hooks without continually dulling the machine's cutting blades. Without proper production equipment, this innovative new product could not be broadly marketed. It took de Mestral twenty years to develop a cutting blade that could handle production runs of Velcro hook and loop fasteners.

Innovative, New Applications

Today, Velcro fasteners are used in ways its inventor couldn't have imagined. They have replaced nails for some uses, and they have been embraced by the apparel industry as ideal fasteners for jackets, sneakers, and wallets, since they do not jam, break, or rust. Velcro fasteners have replaced snaps, zippers, and buttons for many uses; fashion designers like Velcro's versatility.

As stronger fibers have been developed, a whole new range of applications have emerged. NASA's Space Shuttle program uses Velcro on the bottom of astronauts' shoes to keep them from floating around in the cabin when they are in space and to anchor items in astronauts' living quarters.

De Mestral, whose curiosity led him to the discovery of the principle behind Velcro, died in 1990, but his idea has assumed a life of its own. Velcro fasteners are now manufactured in a variety of materials, including polyester, glass fiber, Teflon, and even stainless steel. Because Velcro is lightweight, doesn't rattle, rust or corrode, and has a tendency to adhere more tightly with vibration—rather than coming loose—it is becoming increasingly popular with automotive manufacturers. Velcro fastens bumpers, door panels, seat covers, carpets, and floor mats in cars and trucks. According to the company, Velcro materials are even used to keep artificial hearts in place.

A Breakthrough Invention

Not long ago, a group of international inventors voted Velcro fasteners as one of the fifty most important inventions of the twentieth century. This revolutionary product is used in applications that are limited only by the imagination of its users.

Do we all have de Mestral's ability to, as Thomas Edison said, recognize opportunity when it comes dressed in overalls and looks like work? How many millions of people had picked cockleburs from their clothing before this single individual saw something that wasn't there. Can we learn how better to use our brain and our imagination? A few leading thinkers believe so, and they are proving it in a variety of ways.

A Personal Experience

In 1981, when our daughter Amy was born with hydrocephalus, we had no idea what the term meant or how she would be affected by it. When we questioned neurosurgeons at Children's Memorial Hospital in Chicago, they attempted to explain the disease and the prognosis in terms we could understand.

They used a CAT scan, a computer enhanced three-dimensional X-ray, to illustrate the problem. Because she was two months premature, she was so tiny that the only clothes that fit her were doll clothes. When she had her first surgery, she weighed just over three pounds and her head was about the size of an orange. The doctor pointed to the halves of her brain compressed by the cerebrospinal fluid buildup. Each half was about the size of a grape.

An Atrophied Brain

As gently as he could, the doctor told me that her brain had been prohibited from growing normally because of the fluid accumulation, and that it was hopelessly atrophied. In all likelihood, she would be severely retarded and would probably never walk. The only ray of hope he offered was that little was known about the development of the brain and that particularly in infants it is possible for the brain to grow.

Soon afterward, by remarkable coincidence, Amy shared the intensive care ward with a hospital surgeon's son who had suffered a concussion in a fall. As we exchanged hopes and fears with the boy's mother during our late-night vigil, she told us about the Institute for the Advancement of Human Potential in Philadelphia. It was operated by Glen Doman, a man who was doing remarkable things with brain-damaged children.

Grasping at Straws

We grasped this tiny straw of hope, read Doman's books, and conferred with the Institute. Their advice: Stimulate the child's senses as much as possible to encourage brain development. With nothing to lose and everything to gain, we seized the opportunity. Amy was subjected to a daily barrage of every imaginable kind of stimuli. Merrilee invented a touch board adorned with items that ranged from sandpaper to wool, we showed her paintings and photographs constantly, and the twins' room reverberated with the strains of music that ranged from Mozart to Merle Haggard.

A couple of years later, when Amy was back in the hospital for a less severe problem, once again we reviewed the CAT scans with the neurosurgeon. When he compared the current scans to those when she was first born, the doctor was incredulous, unwilling to accept what his eyes told him until he verified the results. When he was finally satisfied that these were both Amy's scans, he said, "If someone told me these were CAT scans from the same child, I would not have believed it. What we see here today is the brain of a normal child."

"A Normal Child"

Amy's brain had indeed grown until it completely filled the inside of her head, and she has continued to develop normally. In the 1992–93 school year, on the basis of her fourth grade teacher's recommendation and intelligence tests conducted at the end of the year, she entered her school's extended opportunities (gifted) program for fifth graders.

I don't know for sure how much of her development can be attributed to her mother's tireless efforts to stimulate her senses during those critical early years, how much is genetic, and how much is blind luck. But I do know we are all capable of far more that we believe, and I learned that it is possible for our brains to grow and develop in ways we do not fully understand.

An Incredible Organ

The brain is an incredible organ. Says *Psychology Today*, "By far the most sophisticated machine known to man, the adult brain massively outperforms today's best supercomputer. It processes billions of operations a second—approximately ten to the fifteenth power, versus a mere ten to the ninth power for the machine—all in three pounds of tissue crammed inside the cranium."[2]

There is a good argument for the belief that the brain, like our muscles, needs to be exercised regularly to stay fit and trim. In 1991, using a battery of sophisticated tests, UCLA neurologist John Mazziotta, M.D., conducted a series of experiments in an attempt to determine exactly how the brain processes information. Subjects were first asked to sign their names while the researcher monitored brain activity. Not surprisingly, this routine task was completed without much effort on the part of the brain.

Next, Mazziotta asked his subjects to sign their names using their nondominant hand. This time the brain went bonkers.

---

[2]Beth Livermore, "Build a Better Brain," *Psychology Today* (September/October 1992), 42.

Multiple circuits were required to process this unusual request. After several attempts at completing the task, the brain settled down and eventually transferred the job from one area of the brain to another that required less space and energy.

How Learning Works

The good doctor theorized that this pattern represented learning. When a task is learned, the brain—being the incredibly efficient organ it is—shifts the processing from regions of the brain that require more energy to those that operate more automatically. This frees up the most sophisticated parts of the brain to process more complicated and challenging tasks.

Other researchers have found that kids who practice math skills improve learning in other ways. A thorough knowledge of the basics frees up larger portions of their brain for more sophisticated applications. Sometimes the results have been spectacular. Most of us, for example, can remember about seven numbers when a string of numbers are read to us, but after several months' practice, one student learned to remember as many as eighty digits in correct order.

Experiments have shown that memory exercises not only help us recall the information we are studying at the time, but that exercising our brains in one subject area improves our recollection of other types of information, as well. In other words, memorizing math facts may well improve your recall of state capitals or parts of speech. Says Douglas Herrmann, Ph.D., author of *Super Memory*, "If you want to have information at your fingertips, practice remembering it."

Psychology Today goes on to say that scientists have concluded that your diet affects your IQ, your sense of smell stimulates your memory, and that people who can minimize stress through exercise or meditation have better short-term memory, have faster reaction times, and are more creative.[3]

[3]Livermore, 40–47.

Finding the Creative Spark

I've spent a good number of years trying to figure out a way to separate people who have a creative spark from those who don't. In communications, where one's success depends on an ability to make ordinary things interesting, creativity is essential. Virtually anyone with normal intelligence can learn the mechanics of writing and graphic design, but it doesn't mean that what they produce will be imaginative and creative. I've worked with a great number of journalists, for example, who understand very well the principles of writing: how to collect facts, arrange them in proper sequence, get quotes from the right sources, and make the story credible and believable. What they haven't learned is how to make it interesting. Their writing is as dull as dishwater.

I've never figured out how to edit their work or to advise such writers. Because they evaluate their work on application of the mechanics, it won't improve with revision. An editor can send them back for additional research and rewrites endlessly, and they will come back with more facts, but the story will still be dull.

I finally decided that the only way to identify creative people in the hiring process is try to determine if they possess curiosity. If they are innately curious about how things work, what makes people tick, or if they like to find a better way to do things, they will probably be creative in their work.

Everyone Is Potentially Creative

Of course, creativity is not limited to artists, writers, composers, inventors, and other strange personality types (who pride themselves on their eccentricity) in so-called creative occupations and professions. In its most basic sense, creativity is simply the ability to look at things in a unique or unusual way, to find a new way to do something, or to find a new twist for an old idea. We *all* have the *potential* to be creative.

Creativity is not some sort of "elitist ivory tower enterprise," says David N. Perkins, codirector of Harvard University's Project Zero study of cognitive skills in the sciences and humanities. Speaking at a symposium sponsored by the Smithsonian Institution a few years ago, Perkins said there is also a danger in equating creativity with intelligence, talent, and expertise. "These traits are simply the horsepower that fuels the creative process," he said.[4]

Traits of Creative People

There are traits, however, that seem to drive creative people. Perkins and other theorists have identified at least six. They believe the more of these traits you have, the more creative you are likely to be. The six are:

1. A deep concern for hidden truths. Creative people are always searching for opportunities to extract order from chaos. They find beauty in symmetry.

2. They are motivated as much by "problem finding as by problem solving." Former Librarian of Congress Daniel Boorstin told the symposium, "Creators don't quite know what they're seeking—They are exploring the unknown."

3. Creative types delight in challenging assumptions. They are iconoclasts. Perhaps they find purpose and meaning in the very definition of iconoclasm: "the attacking or overthrow of established or venerated institutions, practices, or attitudes."

4. They test the validity of their own ideas. Perhaps because they challenge others, they tend to be more objective about their own. Nobel Prize winning chemist Linus Pauling is said to have told a student that the trick to having good ideas is to come up with "a lot of ideas and then throw the bad ones out." Author Mike Lavelle once told me that he gets book ideas by going to the library, looking on the shelf, and writing a book that is not there.

5. Creative people have their own "intrinsic motivation." They are not tempted by rewards that attract others. They are more interested in new ideas than in money and power. They are innately curious.

---

[4]David M. Maxfield, Smithsonian News Service, "Creative Minds Discuss Roots of Great Ideas," *Providence Journal Bulletin* (January 10, 1988), B1+.

6. Original thinkers work at the edge of their competence. Concert pianist Rosalyn Tureck told the symposium about an almost mystical creative breakthrough she experienced shortly before her seventeenth birthday. When she told her teacher how she arrived at this newfound understanding about the structure of Bach's music, the teacher responded that what she was trying to achieve was "wonderful but impossible to do." Nevertheless, she worked at it for years until she perfected the technique that led to an entirely new way of performing. Knowledge in and of itself is not power. It is only potential power. You have to take action before anything comes of a good idea.

The Idea Is the Easy Part

In fact, many experts believe that what you do after you have a flash of genius is as important as the idea itself. Masco Corporation's director of new products and technology, Dennis O'Connor, tells inventors that inventing a new product is the easy part. "Inventors who have the business savvy to take inventions through development, prototype, manufacturing, marketing and distribution are pretty rare," he says.[5]

De Mestral's experience with Velcro hook and loop fasteners attests to O'Connor's belief. The inventor came up with the idea in an afternoon, and he perfected it in a short time. But it required two decades to figure out how to make the equipment for production runs of the material.

Despite the personal characteristics creative people seem to share, the Smithsonian symposium panelists agreed that creativity is not simply a matter of following the steps as one would follow a recipe to bake a cake. The process is a lot messier and more imprecise. Thoughts are often jumbled, fragmented, stirred, sorted, and reexamined, and may require years to reach their final form.

---

[5]Marc Sneden, "Inspired Inventors! How They Differ from Ordinary Mortals," *The Masco Entrepreneur* 3:1 (1992), 6.

Developing an Idea

The creative process that the symposium panel identified is essentially the same one that James Webb Young discussed in his book, *A Technique for Producing Ideas*, published more than fifty years ago. Young had a five point system:

1. Gather the raw materials. Research the immediate problem and apply information that comes from constant enrichment of your store of general knowledge.
2. Work this information over in your mind.
3. Incubate the idea in your subconscious.
4. Recognize the "Eureka! I've got it!" stage when the idea is actually being born.
5. Shape and develop the idea for practical usefulness.[6]

The creative process usually requires solitude, as well. Seldom do really useful and creative ideas emerge from a committee structure. Most creative people do their best work alone. William H. Whyte, Jr., author of *The Organization Man*, said "People very rarely think in groups; they talk together, they exchange information, they adjudicate, they make compromises. But they do not think; they do not create."[7]

Set Aside Thinking Time

Positive thinker W. Clement Stone has for years advocated spending at least a half hour and perhaps up to two hours every day doing nothing but thinking and reflecting. Such personal study time is essential to stretching the mind and opening it to new ideas. Normal daily activities tend to impede the creative process because of the noise and clutter they generate. Creativity is quiet, it is relaxed, and it is personal.

---

[6]Rance Crain, "Can't Sleep? It's Genius Calling," *Crain's Chicago Business* (June 25, 1984), 10.
[7]Ruth Holladay, "The Creative Mind," *Indianapolis Star*, 24 June 1988, H1+.

The creative process usually requires the mind to be restful and relaxed. Ideas that have incubated in the subconscious for days, weeks, or even years, often emerge only after you allow your mind to rest. That's why you sometimes awaken in the middle of the night with a flash of inspiration. It's a good idea to keep a pencil and notepad nearby for such occasions. Write down ideas that come to you when you are half-asleep so you will remember them, then analyze them the next day in the cold gray light of dawn. If the ideas still seem sound, initiate the final step of shaping them for practical application.

An Approach That Works

When I first began to study this approach some years ago in connection with a book I was working on with W. Clement Stone, I confess that I was a little skeptical about the idea. It was a little too mystical for my taste. I preferred to gather the information, study the facts, develop an outline, and write. On one occasion, however, I struggled and struggled with a particular chapter and could not get it to come together. Finally, I gave up and decided to take a nap, and when I awoke, I had the answer.

I have continued to use the process, and I no longer worry about writer's block or whether or not I can understand and write about complex concepts. I know that if I follow the steps: Gather as much information as possible about the subject, study it, incubate it in the subconscious, and then forget about it for awhile, the answer will come. And the work is usually better than it is when I try to force the conclusion before my subconscious mind has worked through the problem and arrived at a solution.

In pursuit of the elusive concept of creativity, all too often the discussion centers around the fun part—the development of an idea—and overlooks the hard work necessary to shape the idea for practical usefulness. While creativity in and of itself is personally satisfying and rewarding, most of us don't have the luxury of thinking great thoughts and flinging them to the masses for implementation and execution. A big part of success hinges on our ability to shape the ideas for other to use them, a discipline that often requires our creative ideas to be tempered with common sense.

Blending Creativity and Practicality

One of Wall Street's longest running success stories, Warren Buffett, has perfected the art of blending creativity and practicality. In the process, he's made many people rich. A $10,000 investment in the Buffet Partnership made in 1956 and reinvested in Buffett's Berkshire Hathaway in 1969 would have been worth $35 million in 1992 after all taxes, fees, and expenses. Before taxes, fees, etc., the investment would be worth $65 million.

At Berkshire's 1992 annual meeting, Buffet told his shareholders, "In many investment organizations, it is customary to substitute top-down analysis for common sense. First, they start with what's going to happen in the universe and then keep narrowing it down. You've got this great averaging of IQs in a largely offsetting fashion. We think that just tends to be nonsense."

Buffet takes great pride that his organization does not use computers or statistical models to develop investment strategies. Instead Berkshire Hathaway tries to follow the investment axiom: focus on what's knowable and important. He tries to predict "how certain people and companies will swim against the current, not "the fluctuations in the current."

Solutions Searching for Problems

He believes that the principal reason people use statistics instead of common sense is merely because they know how. "To a man with a hammer," he says, "every problem looks like a nail." Buffet believes that those who are enthralled with statistical comparisons of an endless number of variables often overlook the simple fact that when you buy stock, you buy part of a business.

Despite his failure to understand why others overlook the obvious in favor of the obscure, Buffet is grateful that they do. "It is quite valuable from our standpoint," he says. "If you're in the sailing business, you'd want to set up a flat-earth scholarship. It reduces competition like you can hardly believe."

A Commonsense Approach

Buffet says he has patterned his commonsense approach after Nobel laureate Thomas Hunt Morgan, best known for his work in genetics. In a field that required the study of enormous amounts of data and sophisticated mathematics to work out genetic patterns, Morgan forbade the use of a calculator in his department at Cal Tech. He figured that if something required a calculator to work out, it wasn't obvious enough.

Buffett believes the way to make money in the stock market is as basic as buying a good company with good management and staying with it, rather than jumping in and out of one stock after another. "If you are right about the business," he says, "you'll be right about your investments over the long term."

Buffet concluded his address to his shareholders by emphasizing the importance of focusing on what is knowable and important, using extraordinary "horse sense" to guide decisions, and taking action. He speculates that when the Buffet era is over at Berkshire and the final results are in, if the fifteen best decisions are eliminated, "it would not be much of a record."

He tells business students that when they graduate they would be better off if they were issued a ticket with twenty punches on it. Every time they make an investment decision, they would use up a punch. "You'll never use up all twenty punches," he says, "if you save them for great ideas."[8]

The greatest idea in the world is nothing more than an intellectual exercise unless it is acted upon.

---

[8]"Buffett: No Computers, And 20 Punches," *Dick Davis Digest* (July 20, 1992), 1–2.

Key Points and Action Items

1. We often fail to recognize opportunity, Thomas Edison said, because it comes in overalls and looks like work. An idea is only the beginning of the development of something useful.

2. It is possible to expand our brains with exercise, just as we can strengthen our muscles. Tests have shown that memorizing one set of facts helps our recall in other subject areas, as well.

3. The best way to find people who have a creative spark is to determine if they possess curiosity. If they are curious about how things work or what makes people tick, they will probably be creative in their work.

4. We all have the potential to be creative. In simplest terms, creativity is simply the ability to look at things in a unique or unusual way, to find a new way to do something, or to find a new twist for an old idea.

7. Creativity is quiet, relaxed, and personal. William H. Whyte, Jr. noted that we do not think in groups. We talk, exchange information, and compromise, but we do not think. You may find that you do your best work alone.

13

The Right Attitude

There is no security on this earth; there is only opportunity.

—Douglas MacArthur

Not long ago, I was in London, Ontario, for a business meeting with my friends at Emco Limited, a leading Canadian building products manufacturing and distribution company. Since the meeting was expected to be short, I planned to go in and out in one day.

I do a good deal of work with Emco and I go there often. It is about a two and one-half hour drive from my home in suburban Detroit, traffic is light, and the scenery is pleasing. However, when Northwest Airlines added London and several other Canadian cities to its AirLink service, I decided to fly instead of drive.

The meeting concluded early so I went to the London airport for the return trip, expecting to check in for the flight, make a few phone calls, and be home in time for dinner. When I arrived at the ticket counter, however, the reservations agent told me that the flight had been canceled because of equipment problems. Northwest offered three alternatives: staying overnight at the airline's expense and taking the first flight out in the morning, riding to Detroit in a chauffeured limousine with a small group of passengers, or renting a car. I chose to rent a car so I could travel at my own pace and stop off for dinner at one of my favorite restaurants along the way.

The drive home was uneventful. The interesting part came when I returned the car to the airport. When I gave the paperwork to the Budget rental agent at Detroit Metro airport, I told the agent that if there was a problem ferrying the car back to London, I might be able to help. I planned to go there again in about a week; if the car hadn't been returned by then, I would be willing to rent it again and drive it back.

A Belligerent Counter Agent

The agent was quite pleasant, but unsure how to handle the transaction since Detroit and London are in different countries, even though they are only about 140 miles apart. Eventually, she phoned her counterpart in London who insisted upon speaking to me. "Why did you take our car out of the country?" she demanded.

"Because my flight was canceled," I responded. "I told you I was dropping the car in Detroit when I rented it."

"You did not," she said. "You told us you were taking it to Toronto. We wouldn't let you take it out of the country."

"Of course I did. Why on earth would I lie to you about my destination?"

"You cannot take our car out of Canada," she insisted.

"Well, it's here. You figure out how to get it back," I responded, returning the phone to the counter agent.

When I looked over the rental contract later, I discovered that the counter agent had noted that I would drop the car in Toronto. She had not listened to what I said (I verified with my traveling companion that I did indeed say Detroit), and I signed the contract without checking the information she had entered in it. It was a perfect formula for a misunderstanding.

An Unhappy Ending

Budget eventually concluded that it would allow me to drop the car, but would charge me a $200 fee. I called my company's travel department manager, who advised me to pay the bill, get out of there before they aggravated me any more, and they would straighten it out with the rental agency. The travel department called our Budget representative, who had for years tried to land our company as a national account. The sales representative promised to take care of the matter. Budget refused to waive the drop charge, but more than six months after I paid the bill issued a $100 certificate to me that can be applied to the next rental.

There will not be a next Budget rental for me. I will choose any other company first, and if there are no rental cars available, I will take a bus. The attitude of a single rental agent ensured that I will never again be a Budget customer. But that's not the worst of it. Not only did she manage to alienate me, she broadcast her uncooperative attitude to several travel professionals who have the ability to influence thousands of other travelers. And, the entire episode was unnecessary. If, instead of being belligerent, the counter person had been positive and helpful, we could have worked out a satisfactory compromise on the spot.

Two Types of People

There seem to be two basic types of people in the world: those who cheerfully do the right thing and give everyone around them a lift, and those who, even when they do the right thing, do it in such a grudging or adversarial way that they ensure that they will never reap any dividends from their actions. It doesn't require a Ph.D. to figure out which group will advance further in an organization, build a successful business or professional practice, or succeed in whatever line of work they choose. And it's all a matter of attitude.

W. Clement Stone so believes in the importance of a Positive Mental Attitude that he made it the linchpin of his philosophy of success. He quickly points out, however, that PMA is defined as the *appropriate* attitude under the circumstances. It is not the naive belief that if you only look on the bright side, everything will work out the way you would like.

PMA is also the absence of a Negative Mental Attitude. A positive attitude has the power to attract the good and the beautiful while a negative attitude repels them, he says. Stone believes that a negative attitude not only ensures that you will not realize your true potential, it robs you of all that makes life worth living.

PMA Is Starting Point of Success

He says, "A Positive Mental Attitude combined with the selection of a specific goal is the starting point to all success. Your world will change whether or not you choose to change it. But, you do have the power to choose its direction. You can select your own targets.

"For centuries, philosophers have been telling us: 'Know thyself.' What we really should be teaching is not knowing and understanding yourself, but realizing that you have the potential within you to reach any goal in life that you desire as long as it doesn't violate the laws of God or the rights of your fellow man.

"What the mind can conceive and believe," Stone maintains, "the mind of man can achieve with PMA. We translate into physical reality the thoughts and attitudes we hold in our minds. We translate thoughts of poverty and failure into reality just as quickly as we do thoughts of riches and success. When our attitude toward ourselves is big and our attitude toward others is generous and merciful, we attract big, generous portions of success to ourselves."[1]

The right attitude toward your career and your life allows you to attack opportunities with zest and enthusiasm. You don't mind putting in a little overtime and giving the extra effort required to do an outstanding job—instead of a mediocre one—because you know the rewards will come.

Having the right attitude also means taking a long view. Success in any endeavour requires an investment. You may be required to labor for years in obscurity before you find the right combination of opportunity and preparation that brings your achievements to the forefront.

The Right Attitude

The correct attitude is one that is internalized, and should not be confused with an outgoing personality (although others do tend to like enthusiastic people). It is, rather, a mixture of

---

[1]Samuel A. Cypert, *Believe and Achieve* (New York: Avon Books, 1991), 25–26.

quiet confidence, enthusiasm for the task at hand, determination, and the knowledge that the opportunity can be capitalized upon if it is approached thoughtfully, positively, and ethically.

The right attitude means doing everything possible to deliver on commitments. If you promise your boss, your client, or a customer that you will do something, you do it, even if it means working overtime with no extra pay to complete the job. The willingness to go the extra mile always pays great dividends. As writer Elbert Green Hubbard observed years ago, "Folks that never do any more than they get paid for, never get paid for any more than they do."

A Small Job That Paid Big Dividends

Several years ago, when I accepted a free-lance assignment to write a product brochure, I knew that the deadline would require me to work over the weekend that Merrilee and I would be moving out of our apartment into our first home. Although I had not had much experience in real estate transactions, the purchase seemed relatively uncomplicated. In order to move out of our apartment when the lease ended, the sellers had agreed to allow us to move in a few days early. We would pay rent until the closing of the deal.

Things didn't work out as planned. When we arrived at our new home in a rented truck with everything we owned, we found the previous owners still very much present. They had decided it would cost too much to complete some of the repairs that the mortgage lender insisted upon and had decided not to go through with the sale. A few hasty calls to attorneys netted an agreement to meet the following week to work out a satisfactory arrangement, but in the meantime, Merrilee and I had nowhere to go.

Saturday evening found us in a cheap motel—the only room available for miles around—and most of our possessions in storage. When I sat down at a folding table with my typewriter and a stack of paper to write the brochure, Merrilee assumed that I'd taken total leave of my senses. The strain had been too much.

Keeping a Commitment

"Why don't you call your client and explain the situation? No one in his right mind would expect you to finish that job under the circumstances," she said.

"I know," I said. "But, I don't have his home phone number. Besides, I couldn't bear the thought of my client having to face his client empty-handed on Monday morning. He's counting on the brochure for an important meeting, and the writing must be completed this weekend to make the printing deadline. I have to do it."

"You're nuts," she said.

"I know," I sighed.

The story has a happy ending. The client loved the brochure, the problems with the home sale were worked out quickly, and soon after these events transpired, my client heard about an opening at Peat Marwick for a position that seemed to be a good match for my background and experience. "Cypert is the most reliable, most committed person I know," my client told the executive recruiter in charge of the search.

I got the job and a thirty percent increase in salary. A string of regular promotions followed, and I was transferred to Peat's headquarters in New York where I eventually headed up communications for the entire firm. I credit the chain of events that led to this success to my determination to meet commitments, regardless of the inconvenience to me personally.

Start by Doing What You Like

Developing the appropriate attitude begins with doing something you like to do. If you are stuck in a dull job with no future, it is hard to get excited about the possibilities. On the other hand, if you so enjoy your work that you look forward to getting started every day, it is natural that you will approach it much more positively.

In truth, however, there probably is no perfect job. Each comes with its share of tedious tasks that you would rather not do and coworkers you would rather not be around. The happiest people in any position are those who view the job description as a summary of minimum standards to be met. They perform what is expected of them and much, much more.

They delight in finding a faster, better way to perform mundane chores in order to get them over with so they can go on to more interesting things. Such positive people are always on a quest for continuous improvement in everything they do. Because they are busy, industrious, and dependable, they are rewarded with more and more work, and they get it done.

These achievers operate well at any level in an organization. If they are senior executives, they motivate everyone around them to challenge themselves to work harder, to accomplish more. If they are lower on the ladder, they persuade others to help them. They sell their ideas and enlist support for their projects. And they climb the ladder quickly. Virtually every organization has a shortage of motivated self-starters who like their work, attack it enthusiastically, and inspire everyone around them to run faster and jump higher.

Their enthusiasm is infectious. Others like being around them and working with them. They make boring jobs exciting. They have a sense of purpose that seems to confer more importance on their projects than they really merit. They are in a hurry to complete a task so they can move on to the next one.

Developing Enthusiasm

Can such enthusiasm be learned or is it a personality trait that you either have or you don't? The answer, W. Clement Stone says, is an unequivocal yes; it can be learned, and it can be generated at will. He says that the word itself implies that in fact the only source of enthusiasm is yourself. Enthusiasm is derived from the Greek *en* (within) and *Theos* (God). Thus, enthusiasm means "God within us," he says.

"The emotions are not always subject to reason," Stone points out, "but they are always immediately subject to action (mental or physical). Furthermore, repetition of the same thought or physical action develops into a habit which when repeated frequently enough becomes an automatic reflex.

"That's why I use self-motivators. A self-motivator is an affirmation . . . self command . . . platitude . . . or any symbol that you deliberately use as self-suggestion to move yourself to desirable action. You merely repeat a verbal self-motivator fifty times in the morning and fifty times at night for a week or ten days to imprint the words indelibly in your memory."

The application of this technique, Stone says, has the effect of allowing you to recall instantly key self-motivators when you need them most. He believes that in order to be enthusiastic, you have to act enthusiastic. When you take sincere action to express your inner enthusiasm, you accentuate the power of suggestion and self-suggestion. Because you *act* enthusiastic, you *become* enthusiastic.

His favorite list of self motivators includes:

- God is always a good God!
- You have a problem . . . that's good!
- With every adversity there is a seed of an equivalent or greater benefit.
- What the mind can conceive and believe, the mind can achieve.
- Find one good idea that will work and . . . work that one good idea!
- Do it now!
- To be enthusiastic . . . Act enthusiastically![2]

Don't Accept Restrictions

A Positive attitude can help you overcome incredible obstacles. For much of his early life, Phil Fuentes was told more about what he could not do than what he could do. Finally, he says, he just stopped asking. "I have found throughout my life that my only restrictions were those that were placed upon me by other people," he says.

Fuentes knows from painful personal experience what he's talking about. Born in 1956 with cerebral palsy, he was told by doctors, guidance counselors, and other well-meaning professionals that he would never live a "normal" life. Because of the disease's effect on his muscles, even simple tasks like tying his shoes and necktie were difficult, often agonizing experiences for Fuentes. He had to have special instruction to

---

[2] W. Clement Stone, "The Little Difference That Makes the Big Difference," *Success Unlimited* (November 1967), 2–4.

learn motor skills that most of us take for granted.

Fortunately, Fuentes was blessed with an abundance of stubborn determination. When others told him that he could not do something, he redoubled his efforts until he proved them wrong. Over a cup of coffee in his restaurant in suburban Chicago, he told me about playing softball, football, and other physical sports with his brothers and other kids in his neighborhood on Chicago's tough Southwest Side. ''I wasn't great,'' he recalls, ''and I was almost always the last one chosen, but I played. When I couldn't catch the ball in a glove, I used a fishing net.''

Making His Own Choices

When his doctor told him he wouldn't be able to ride a bike, but that there were more important things in life anyway, Fuentes decided on the spot that from that day forward he alone would decide what was important to him and what was not. Only he would be allowed to place restrictions upon himself. No one else could. He was in sixth grade before he learned to ride a bike, but he can ride one today.

Ditto with high school R.O.T.C. When school officials at Steinmetz High discouraged his joining the R.O.T.C. program he brushed aside their objections, and eventually advanced to the rank of major. He tried out for the drill team and made it despite his inability to straighten his right arm. In competitions he wore a splint so judges would think he was injured instead of handicapped.

Fuentes was so angry with the driver's license examiner who placed a restriction on his license that he must only drive vehicles with power steering that he borrowed a friend's car with manual steering to prove to the State of Illinois that he could drive any type of vehicle he wished. Even though his own automobile had power steering and he was unlikely to drive one without it, he was unwilling to accept any limitation whatsoever. He got the restriction lifted.

No Limitations

He was equally unwilling to accept limitations on the job. He worked his way through college as an Andy Frain usher and parking attendant, earning his associate degree in accounting from Wright Junior College and his BA in business and economics from Northeastern University. Fuentes is proud that he was the only United Airlines sky cap with an MBA. An MBA was a personal goal, he says, to prove to himself and no one else that he could do it, although he figured the marketing expertise he gained from his studies would be a valuable asset in any business.

The people skills he learned in those service jobs, combined with his formal education, provided the foundation for a business career. The money he had invested in the stock market as he held down two and three jobs provided the capital he needed to realize his dream of becoming a McDonald's owner/operator.

It wasn't easy. Fuentes figures some twenty thousand people annually apply for about one hundred available franchises. "In a way, though," he says, "this is no different from anything else I've done. All my life people have been telling me, 'you can't do this and you can't do that.' I knew I could run a McDonald's. When I went for my interview, I knew it was my big chance and I wasn't going to blow it. I talked to them for hours and I assured them that there were no physical or mental limitations that could keep me from being an outstanding McDonald's owner/operator.

Positive Attitude Pays Off

"When it was over, the interviewer told me, 'I have other candidates with more money and better experience than you, but I think you will make a good operator, so we are going to start you in the training program,'" Fuentes said. His determined positive attitude had once again prevailed.

He worked as a computer consultant and part-time skycap to support his family while completing McDonald's two-year training program in working stores to learn the practical aspects of running a successful franchise. To no one's surprise, Fuentes sailed through the training program with colors flying.

Today, he presides over the Sanders Court McDonald's at the corner of Dundee and Sanders Roads in Northbrook, Illinois, an affluent suburb of Chicago. Fuentes takes great pride in the fact that most of his employees are Hispanic. He's helped them learn to speak English and earn their United States citizenship, and he serves by example as a positive role model. "Attitude is what it's all about," he says. "You can't expect people to be positive all the time. It wouldn't be normal. Every once in a while you need someone to shake you up a little. The important thing is to keep your eye on the final goal.

A Goal-oriented Operation

"We are very goal oriented here. I get everyone from the grill person to the manager of the store involved. Everyone has a say in the goals. We are open to suggestion on any aspect of our business. The person in any particular job is the one that is best qualified to make recommendations for making the job more enjoyable or more efficient.

"We have an open door policy here where people are always told that they are welcome to come in with suggestions at any time. I try to listen to every suggestion, find the good points, and take into account any drawbacks of which they might not be aware. I help them shape their ideas for practical application," Fuentes says.

He is a strong proponent of promoting from within and usually has four or five people participating in McDonald's management development program. To help workers develop and maintain their positive attitudes, on birthdays and other special occasions he gives them a Spanish-language copy of Napoleon Hill's classic *Think and Grow Rich*. He encourages them to practice the principles of success that Hill outlined in his bestselling book, and he rewards outstanding performance with a variety of other incentives.

Employees are given tickets to ball games, passes to Great America theme park, and dinner gift certificates. Because he has more adults than teenagers working in his store, rewards usually include employees and their families in order to make the event more meaningful. When his restaurant received high marks on a full field inspection, Fuentes hosted a dinner for the entire management team at which the top performer was recognized.

Overcoming Obstacles

Fuentes knows from his own experience the importance of attitude in overcoming obstacles. He believes it is important to assess one's strengths and weaknesses realistically, to build on the strengths and work on weaknesses. "Your strengths are what you have to let people know about," he says. "Sell yourself with all you have in the beginning. Then work on your weaknesses. Knowing what my weaknesses are, I have tried to continually improve on them. If you improve a little every day, eventually that weakness becomes a strength."

Fuentes also believes that helping others less fortunate greatly assists in building a positive attitude. He is active in charity work, particularly with children who have special needs or are disabled. "It really hurts me when I see a handicapped child and their parents don't encourage them to try different things—they shelter them too much. In order to succeed you have to be able to succeed in society at large.

"When I was a kid, I went to a special school until the second grade when my parents decided that if I'm going to make it in the real world, I am going to have to adapt. I was lucky that they had the strength to pull me out of the special education school and put me into the mainstream.

"Of course this approach may not be right for everybody. My problems are not that severe. But a kid in a wheelchair doesn't necessarily need to stay out of a regular school or never try things with other kids. Any kid is going to fall and get hurt. That's part of growing up. The important thing is that everyone has his or her own personality and needs and you have to find the right balance *for them*. The way society is, you have to let people work out their own problems and fit in their own way."

Take a Break

Fuentes recognizes that everyone—including himself—has a bad day now and again. When it starts to wear on him, he pauses to reflect, finding solace in the knowledge that "tomorrow's another day. I know that's cliché, but I just accept the fact that today is a bad day. Sometimes I stop whatever I am doing and just take a break—go home and play with the kids for a while.

"If you step away from a bad situation for even a couple of hours, it helps," he says. "You can come back the next day and face the problem, recognize what has happened and find a solution or determine what you can do to keep the situation from recurring. Nothing is really as bad twenty-four hours later as it first seemed. That's why it is a good idea not to make hasty decisions, especially if you are in a bad mood.

"We are in the people business. Because I'm the boss, I have to be 'up' every day. When I walk in the front door, everyone looks at me. If I were in a bad mood, it would ruin the day for everyone else. I like to start the day by getting everyone to smile. I find out how they are doing. We may not end the day the same way, but I know that in the morning I can get a laugh from an employee or a smile from a customer.

Selling Others on Positive Thinking

"I recognize that it's human nature to look at the negatives more than the positives, but when it comes to my employees, I have to decide if they have enough positive attributes that make it worthwhile for me to work with them, to help them develop, to become a member of our management team. I'm happy to say that all the salaried workers who were here when I took over the restaurant from the previous owner have stayed with me. We have turned the operation around. It's a more fun place to work, and we have a more positive attitude among members of the management team. It was my responsibility to sell them. Like anything else, people can't be forced into accepting my beliefs. They have to be sold. They have to buy into the program and be willing to work as a team."

Because of his unflagging determination and his stubborn refusal to accept less than the best from himself, Fuentes has inspired countless others. His relentless good humor in the face of adversity has encouraged those who might have given up hope to get up, dust themselves off, and give it another try. As the professionals warned many years ago, Phil Fuentes did not grow up to be "normal." He grew up to be exceptional.

Key Points and Action Items

1. There are two types of people in the world: those who cheerfully do the right thing and give everyone around them a lift and those who somehow find a way to do it wrong even when they do the right thing. Choose to work with positive people, whatever your position may be.

2. A Positive Mental Attitude combined with a definite goal is the starting point of all success. You can't keep your world from changing, but you can choose its direction.

3. Always go the extra mile to deliver on your commitments. As Elbert Hubbard noted, "Folks that never do any more than they get paid for, never get paid for any more than they do."

4. Enthusiasm can be learned. It can only be generated from within. When you act enthusiastic, you become enthusiastic. The emotions may not always be subject to reason, but they are always subject to action.

5. Follow Phil Fuentes's example. Never let others place restrictions upon you that you are unwilling to accept. Decide for yourself what is important to you and what is not. Keep your eye on your final goal.

14

Building Relationships

Be nice to people on your way up
because you'll meet them on your way down.

—WILSON MIZNER

Every few weeks Marty Edelston organizes a special dinner in New York City. The publisher of *Boardroom Report* and *The Bottom Line* newsletter, among others, Edelston invites contributors to his publications, authors of recently published books, business and civic leaders, foreign diplomats, and just plain interesting people.

Caterers proffer exotic dishes, the wine is good and plentiful, and the atmosphere is extraordinary. Guests chat about great events of the day amid bookshelves stuffed with new releases and old favorites or pause to admire a painting or other work of art. The setting is carefully designed—including seating arrangements at dinner—to encourage the exchange of ideas among an eclectic assortment of original thinkers.

The experience is so exhilarating that participants are often reluctant to leave. Conversations continue in the hallway, down the elevator, and in front of the building until the taxis come and whisk the people away. Many friendships have sprung up as a result of one of "Marty's dinners." Edelston has found a very good formula for keeping himself up-to-date on what is going on in the world by creating a social setting that encourages dialogue among people who otherwise might never meet each other.

His forum for the exchange of ideas is an example of what can happen when intelligent, motivated achievers get together, and it is a model that anyone can adopt. When a group of compatible, like-minded people work together on a *permanent* basis, they build upon the type of intellectual synergy that Edelston facilitates, and they develop an emotional commitment to each other that allows them to achieve incredible results. We read about their successes in newspapers and magazines, and we see them on television talking about their latest achievement.

A Master-Mind Alliance

It is what Napoleon Hill called a "Master-Mind Alliance," a term he credits to Andrew Carnegie, who he says was the originator of the idea. According to Hill, although Carnegie founded the company that became the giant U.S. Steel, he knew very little about the intricacies of the steel business. He saw his greatest value as his ability to assemble a team of outstanding individuals and create an environment in which they could succeed.

Hill defined a Master-Mind Alliance as "two or more minds working together in perfect harmony toward a common goal." His description is that of the highest form of networking, the ultimate intellectual relationship with another person. When such an alliance is created, the capability of the group expands exponentially. The combined strengths of the group are far more powerful than the sum of each individual contribution.

Relationships operate at intellectual and emotional levels, but the most powerful are those in which members of the group are in agreement intellectually and are emotionally committed to the success of the entire group. Even the highest form of teamwork may vary in intensity. Most of us are more committed to our lovers, spouses and families, for example, than to our coworkers, but each is important to our success.

Levels of Relationships

Objectives in a relationship may be temporarily shared or they may represent lifetime commitments. We wouldn't expect to have a long-standing friendship with a salesclerk, for example. The only thing we have in common is that we wish to buy something, and he or she wants to sell it to us. Better managed companies, however, recognize that relationships are the most important part of the business and that they can be strengthened if they are managed properly. Their goal is to establish an ongoing relationship with us by giving us good service, quality products, and competitive prices. We respond by developing loyalty to a particular store, salesperson, brand—or in the best case, to all three.

In the achievement of our goals, we have many relationships at many levels, and different expectations for each. We expect our family's encouragement, counsel, and unflagging support, while we expect our coworkers simply to carry out their responsibilities to the best of their ability. Our relationship with them is built upon a temporarily shared objective. It's much like a sports team in which each player has a role in the overall outcome of the game, but when it's over, each goes his or her separate way.

The Leader's Job: Build Commitment

In any business endeavor, as in any team effort, it is the job of the coach, the leader, the manager, or the entrepreneur to persuade or inspire others to align their goals with his. If things work as they should, it is a relationship from which everyone benefits, and if the deal is correctly structured at the outset, each person involved benefits according to the time, effort, and money he or she has invested in the venture.

It isn't necessary to be the boss to be a leader. Management is about increasing the value of the assets with which you have been entrusted; leadership is about inspiring others to work together toward a common goal. It is possible to do both, but such people are exceedingly rare today.

When you know what you wish to accomplish with your life, when you set goals for yourself, you automatically assume a leadership role, regardless of your "official" position within the group. If you have the courage of your convictions, if you have thought through the group's objectives, the chances are good that you are already ahead of the rest of the group. By taking the initiative, you have become a *de facto* leader.

Persuading people to cooperate with each other and to support your team's goals may be the most difficult part of any undertaking, but it is virtually impossible to succeed without the active, enthusiastic, positive support and encouragement of others. Harald Kessler, senior partner of Peat Marwick International's Continental European practice, saw firsthand the importance of a team's attitude in the late 1980s when his firm merged with Klynveld Main Goerdeler.

Change Demands Leadership

Times of great change in a business call for strong, steady leadership, perhaps more than at any other time in the life of an organization. Kessler observed, "Life is all about change, and being successful in business is all about change. It means adapting to change and environments that change. There will always be those who can adapt faster and those who adapt less well."[1]

It is the job of a leader, Kessler believes, to get the members of the team on board during such times. Regardless of the nice packaging and incentives aimed at encouraging others to join us in our effort, what it really comes down to is leadership. A true leader is one who is able to create something that inspires others to identify with it, to conform their own objectives to those of the organization or group. The objective doesn't have to be worked out in minute detail, but it does have to be clear in the minds of members of the group who are striving to reach it.

It doesn't require a complex mission statement or a vision statement with a lot of stilted business language. In fact, the simpler it is, the better it is likely to work. Neither does it require a shelf of manuals or policies and procedures books. What it does require is a committed team whose members

---

[1]Samuel A. Cypert, *Following The Money* (New York: AMACOM Books, 1991), 154.

respect each individual on the team for his or her contribution to the overall effort, people who show by personal example—not by words and speeches—that they care about the team.

The group begins to approach its potential when each member aligns his or her personal objectives with those of the team and makes an emotional commitment to its success. When each person clearly understands his role, believes that each individual will succeed if the team succeeds, benefits according to his contribution, and trusts the team's leader, the results can be astounding.

The Wal-Mart Example

Sam Walton built one of America's most successful retail chains by following precisely this formula. In the late 1960s, when Sam and his brother Bud had about twenty Wal-Marts, a union tried to organize two of his stores in Missouri. Sam retained labor lawyer John Tate, now an executive vice president of Wal-Mart, to help him. Tate related his conversation with Walton to *Fortune* magazine. "You can approach this one of two ways," he said. "Hold people down and pay me or some other lawyer to make it work. Or devote time and attention to proving to people you care."[2]

Walton, of course, chose the latter approach. It was about that time that he began calling his employees associates, and he gave them a piece of the action. He shared detailed financial information with hourly department managers and set specific goals for each store. If they exceeded their goal, he shared the additional profit with them. He also gave them a bonus for minimizing inventory shrinkage, the plague of retailing. Along the way, he made millionaires of many of his associates and investors. A $1,000 investment in Wal-Mart stock when it went public in 1970 would now be worth about $500,000.

Walton built a company that today has in the neighborhood of 1,750 stores and is adding to that number at a rate of about 150 a year. His phenomenal success made him the richest man in America, a title he hated and eventually shucked by trans-

---

[2] John Huey, "Wal-Mart: Will It Take over the World?" *Fortune* (January 30, 1989), 55.

ferring much of his wealth to his family members. The first time *Fortune* included Wal-Mart in its survey of most admired corporations, it tied for ninth place. A year later it had moved up to fifth place, and today it is in third.

Mr. Sam's Style

Images of "Mr. Sam" in his old pickup truck with his dogs in the back or getting a haircut in the same country barbershop that he has patronized for years have become a part of the American consciousness. His down-to-earth style and "aw shucks" demeanor made him a genuine American folk hero. He became the darling of Wall Street and was sought after by the rich and famous, but he remained unchanged by the notoriety he attracted and the billions he earned.

Until he died in 1992 at age seventy-four of leukemia and bone-marrow cancer, Walton maintained his focus right where he thought it should be: on his associates and his customers. He traveled tirelessly, and until the sheer size of the Wal-Mart empire made it impossible, he visited every store at least once a year. When the business became too far-flung to drive to the stores, he bought an airplane and learned to fly it so he could cover more ground faster. He encouraged his officers to maintain the same relentless travel schedule, which resulted in the company's modest headquarters being empty most of the time. All the top executives were out visiting the stores and meeting customers.

Much of Walton's success was the result of his uncanny ability to inspire those around him to work with him to achieve results that even the most optimistic experts thought were impossible. He began his empire in a small town in Arkansas when the conventional wisdom was that a population base of at least 50,000 was required to sustain a discount store. The big chains ignored him at first and often shared information with him simply because he asked. By the time they noticed him, he was well on his way to outgrowing them. As *Fortune* observed, Wal-Mart "has sailed the whole retail industry into uncharted waters and left the old industry giants sitting on the shore wondering where everybody went."[3]

---

[3] John Huey, "America's Most Successful Merchant," *Fortune* (September 23, 1991), 59.

Taking Care of Customers

He didn't worry about recessions or other esoteric things he could do nothing about. He worried about his associates and his customers. He gave his ambitious associates opportunities to manage multimillion dollar operations and created thousands of jobs for new associates. Though he had a well-deserved reputation for being a hard-nosed buyer, a contract with Wal-Mart often made the difference between success and failure for many of his suppliers.

Those he cared for and about repaid him with unflagging loyalty and devotion. Associates pride themselves on giving the best service available anywhere. In his regular visits to Wal-Mart stores, he commended them for their performance and credited them with being the key to Wal-Mart's success. Before he left, he usually led the associates in the Wal-Mart Cheer and if he received sufficient encouragement, he might sing a song over the store's sound system. "It's Hard to Be Humble" was among his favorites.

Like Del Smith of Evergreen Airlines, Walton paid a great deal of attention to how the managers treat associates. It was standard procedure for him to ask them how they liked their store manager or their district manager. If he got an unfavorable response, he assured them that he would take care of it, and he made a note to look into the matter if the response wasn't downright enthusiastic.

Walton took great pains to surround himself with key executives who shared his passion for customer service to ensure that the business would not skip a beat after his death. His values were the company's values, and if his people preserve the legacy he left them, Wal-Mart may well become one of the greatest success stories of the twentieth century.

Ben & Jerry's Homemade, Inc.

Unlike Wal-Mart and its white-haired founder, the move toward employee involvement and teamwork in many companies is driven by entrepreneurs and managers who grew up in the 1960s counterculture and clung to their beliefs as they matured and entered the business world. "Yesterday's flower children have become today's CEOs and they're bringing '60s values into the boardroom,'' according to Carol Clurman, writing in *USA Weekend*.[4] She points to former hippies turned business moguls, Ben Cohen and Jerry Greenfield, both fortyish, as prime examples.

Co-founders of Ben & Jerry's Homemade, Inc., the dynamic duo of the ice-cream world run an unorthodox operation, to be sure. Friends since childhood, Cohen and Greenfield from the outset made a formidable team. They mastered the technique of ''mix-ins'' and displayed a knack for names that link their generational values and their love of ice cream. Heath Bar Crunch, Blueberry Cheesecake, Oreo Mint, and Chocolate Chip Cookie Dough complement Ben & Jerry's ''living flavors,'' Cherry Garcia and Wavy Gravy (named after Woodstock's master of ceremonies).

Institutionalizing Values

They seem to have found a formula that allows each to complement the other's strengths and, like Sam Walton, to institutionalize their personal values. Vice-Chairman Greenfield runs the day-to-day operations of the business as well as Ben & Jerry's charitable foundation. He is reputedly the chief proponent of the company's laid-back style while Chairperson of the Board (yes, that's his formal title) Cohen spends most of his time on the road, promoting the company's business.

It was Greenfield who created the first Ben & Jerry's flavor (their version of vanilla), and when the company was an upstart in the premium ice-cream business, he picketed Pillsbury headquarters to protest what he saw as Pillsbury's Haagen-Dazs subsidiary's attempt to lock them out of the market.

Nevertheless, Greenfield credits Cohen with being the real visionary of the partnership. It was Cohen who figured out how to reconcile the duo's soaring profits with their funda-

---

[4]Carol Clurman, ''More Than Just a Paycheck,'' *USA Weekend* (January 19-21, 1990), 4.

mental mistrust of business with an idea he called "caring capitalism."

"Ben says that business is usually defined as something that produces goods and services," Greenfield told *Rolling Stone* magazine, "but when he looks at a business, he sees a unique combination of human labor and money, and that equals power.[5]

Caring Capitalism

Their caring capitalism is manifested in their social-conscious approach to the company's products, its contributions, and its employees. It sells popsicles called "Peace Pops," contributes profits from its "Rainforest Crunch" to help save the Amazon rain forest, and buys brownies made by unemployed and homeless people in New York and blueberries picked by Native Americans in Maine.

When milk prices dropped as a result of weakening federal price support programs, the company continued to pay Vermont dairy farmers above market prices for milk. Cohen said, "We refuse to profit off the misfortune of our dairy suppliers due to some antiquated, misguided, convoluted federal system."[6]

Employees help choose the causes that receive contributions of 7.5 percent of Ben & Jerry's pretax profits, and they are evaluated in part by their commitment to the company's social causes. They also benefit from Ben & Jerry's commitment to their employees. Production workers have a say in the tasks they will perform every day, they get free back rubs, and every employee gets three free pints of ice cream to take home every day. The company's benefits package includes free health club memberships, profit sharing, college tuition, and day care. The company also has a policy that no one in the company may earn more than seven times the salary of anyone else.

---

[5]Robert E. Sullivan, Jr., "Just Desserts," *Rolling Stone* (July 9-23, 1992), 77.
[6]Daniel Seligman, "Ben & Jerry Save the World," *Fortune* (June 3, 1991), 247.

A Practical Approach

There is a practical side to the Ben & Jerry's approach. With the declining number of people entering the work force and the changes in attitudes, companies are finding new ways to recruit and retain the best workers. Ben & Jerry's has simply raised the stakes a bit by demonstrating that the firm cares about all aspects of its employees' lives and providing perks for all employees, not just the executives.

The renegade ice-cream tycoons have also found favor on Wall Street (despite annual reports with bumper stickers that read: Practice Random Acts of Kindness and Senseless Beauty), thanks to a bottom line that keeps on growing. The company's sales, profits, and stock price are soaring, "baffling critics who predicted the company's super-rich and high-priced ice cream would be a fad. 'For a number of years, it's been like, "They can't do it again," but they do,' says Howard Waxman, editor of an industry newsletter, the *Ice Cream Reporter*."[7]

Recently, Ben & Jerry's has drawn flak from critics who say the company "does not walk its talk." The company has been accused of violating some of the very principles upon which it was founded.[8] Time alone will tell whether the founders stick to their philosophy or Ben & Jerry's becomes "just another unfeeling corporation," but their success is sure to inspire others who believe that an organization prospers most when its members work together for the benefit of the entire group.

As the world becomes increasingly complex and crowded, the ability to work effectively with others will be a critical element of success in business, government, religion, and in personal relationships. Today partnerships between large companies with capital and small entrepreneurial firms with flexibility, speed, and ideas have become a way of life in American business, and universities that competed for students in the

---

[7]Suzanne Alexander, "Life's Just a Bowl of Cherry Garcia for Ben & Jerry's," *Wall Street Journal*, 15 July 1992, B3.

[8]Carolyn Friday, "Cookies, Cream 'n' Controversy: Has Ben & Jerry's Strayed from its Hippie Roots?" *Newsweek* (July 5, 1993), 40.

past have teamed up to offer innovative approaches to education.

The Power of Teamwork

It is not a difficult concept, teamwork, but it is one that some people can never quite get their arms around. I once (briefly, thankfully) worked for a man who prided himself on his team-building skills and didn't hesitate to share that view of himself with others. But his concept of teamwork was roughly this: "Okay, we're a team. I'll be the coach, the captain, and the quarterback, the rest of you block and tackle. If you do a really good job at it, when the game is over, I'll let you carry me off the field on your shoulders."

Of course, he missed the whole point of working with others. To be a successful member of a team requires us to cage our egos, to accept the notion that sometimes we must subvert our own personal desires for the good of the team. Sometimes we run with the ball, sometimes we block and tackle, but it always means giving our best effort to achieve the *group's* goal.

The amazing thing is that when we do, we set in motion a force that not only makes us a better team, it makes us stronger as individuals. We become better, more capable leaders who know when it is our turn to shine and when it is time to let someone else stand in the spotlight. The success of the team reflects upon us all. When we care about other members of the team, we become people that others care about.

When the members of any group—whether it is a company with thousands of employees or a husband and wife team—make a commitment that they will stand or fall together, the group's potential is unlimited.

Key Points and Action Items

1. You can build your own team the way other successful people do—by inspiring others to align their goals with yours. Do so by making sure that everyone involved benefits in proportion to their contribution.

2. You become a *de facto* leader when you set goals for yourself and you know where you are going. Others like to be around those who have a plan for their life and their team.

3. Sam Walton showed it is possible to achieve results others think are impossible by taking care of those you want to care about you. When people know you care, they will reward you in kind.

4. In today's hectic, highly competitive world, if you want others to work with you, you must do more than pay them well. You must also prove that you care about them as people.

5. When you are part of a team, sometimes you get to be the star, and sometimes you get to do the grunt work. Teamwork requires you to control your ego and subvert your personal desires to the team's objectives.

15

Trust, Empowerment, and Delegation

You may be deceived if you trust too much, but you will live in torment if you do not trust enough.

—FRANK CRANE

When Merrilee and I were planning our wedding almost two decades ago, the minister, Reverend Philip Desnes, pastor of Merrilee's church in Deerfield, Illinois, had a strict policy that everyone he married had to come to his office for a prenuptial conference. He talked about the importance of respect and consideration for each other, and he ended the conference with some advice. He said, "In the course of many years in the ministry, I have found that people usually fight about one of three things: money, in-laws, and sex. I hope you have a lot of money and a great sex life because I know your in-laws."

Over the years, we chuckled at his in-law joke and reflected on his wisdom about the topics that usually set off arguments. And even though, intellectually, we knew better, for years afterward, every other Saturday Merrilee and I had an argument about money. It was as predictable as the sunrise in the morning. Sometimes they were small arguments, sometimes they were long, protracted, and bitter, depending upon the circumstances. It was on those Saturdays that we paid our household bills and balanced our checkbook.

We both tried to avoid the arguments, but invariably the exercise would reveal that one of us had made a math error, failed to enter a check in the check register or pay an overdue bill. The result, of course, was that we always had less money than we thought. We shared the same goal: we wished to pay our bills on time, save some money for the future, and maintain a good credit rating. It was a simple plan that was incredibly difficult to execute.

Trial and Mostly Error

During the course of eighteen years of marriage, we tried every technique we could imagine to alleviate the source of the problem. We sought advice from accountants, read books on the subject, developed budgets and spreadsheets, and planned everything in advance. We tried using only one checkbook, only one of us writing checks, never using the bank cash machines, paying the bills together, paying the bills individually, and putting the entire system on computer. Nothing worked to our satisfaction. We still made mistakes—sometimes pretty large ones.

Philosophically, we agreed that managing the household accounts should be Merrilee's job. She was most familiar with the daily activities of everyone in the home and the expenses that were incurred in connection with managing the household. Besides, writing consumed most of my weekends, leaving me very little time to devote to our finances. Invariably, though, she would make an egregious error and I would again seize control of the checkbook.

Straining the Relationship

Eventually, the arguments began to strain our relationship beyond the everyday disagreements of two spirited, opinionated people living under the same roof. Our caustic comments hurt each other more than we wished, and we had the same argument over and over with nothing changing as a result. Neither of us wanted this to continue. Finally, it reached the point that if we didn't take some drastic action we would strain our otherwise great relationship beyond repair. Neither of us could understand how we could work out far more serious problems than these, yet were seemingly unable to come to grips with managing our finances.

One bill-paying Saturday, as I reflected upon our disagreement, I was struck by the silliness of it all. We had argued about the same topic for so long that each knew what the other was going to say before we said it. It was pointless. Neither of us was going to change. The only way we could alleviate the problem was for us to accept each other the way we were or to split up. The latter option was unacceptable, but analyzing the situation in such stark terms made me realize how close we had come too many times in the past.

As I reflected on the situation and the options available to me, the decision was easy. My marriage was worth far more to me than my credit rating. I would turn the accounts over to Merrilee and trust her to manage them. If she didn't do it well, she would have to deal with the consequences. I would no longer review her work and question her methods. It would be her responsibility, and hers alone. If she asked for my advice, I would give it. If she didn't, I would stay out of it.

A Transformation

I never discussed my decision with Merrilee, but almost immediately a transformation took place in both of us. I felt as though a great burden had been lifted from me. I had considered the ultimate consequences and decided I could live with them. Whatever happened, as far as I was concerned, it would be better than what we had been doing. My actions must have conveyed my new attitude, because Merrilee immediately rose to the occasion. She recorded every check, paid every bill, balanced the checkbook to the penny, and saved and invested more than we ever had before.

If someone had predicted this outcome, I would never have believed it. My forecast was much more pessimistic. I expected Merrilee to make many mistakes that would cause us enormous problems, but she didn't. She made a few small mistakes, but she corrected them and went on about her business. She became a disciplined, responsible money manager, and the only thing that had changed was my attitude toward her. I truly trusted her to take charge. So she did.

A Critical Element of Empowerment

That trust is a critical and often overlooked element of the employee empowerment movement that is sweeping American business today. Employees must know that the boss or the owner will help and advise them when they need assistance and stay out of the way when they don't. They must know that when they make mistakes, the company will help them find a solution to the problem without trying to affix blame. Without trust and support from every level of management, empowerment is little more than a clever way for managers to blame employees for everything that goes wrong.

Empowerment is not simply another buzzword in the business lexicon. It is a change in the way a company operates. The company's managers must be leaders, not administrators. They must show by their actions—not their words—that they care about their employees. They must create a corporate culture based upon respect for the contribution of every individual, where people are encouraged to speak their minds without fear of reprisal, and to find newer and better ways to do things. When someone comes up with a better idea, he or she should be recognized and rewarded, and the idea should be implemented, not suffocated by the bureaucracy. If what appeared to be a good idea cannot be implemented for some reason, it should be explained to the person who conceived it.

It really is nothing more than the commonsense application of the Golden Rule. If you treat your employees as you would like to be treated if the roles were reversed—with courtesy and respect—they will respond in kind. Too many managers in corporate America practice what I call the SUDD (suck up, dump down) theory of management. They suck up to the bosses and dump on their employees, because that's the way they were treated when they were at the bottom of the corporate ladder. They learned that was the way the system worked.

A Company Built on Trust

Fred Smith built the giant Federal Express Corporation upon the opposite belief. The company was founded on his firm conviction that ordinary people will do extraordinary things if you believe in them, support them, and simply allow them to excel.

By all logical accounts, Federal Express shouldn't even exist. It was based upon an idea that Smith had at age twenty when he was a student at Yale University. As part of a class assignment, he wrote a research paper on the subject of an overnight freight company based on the hub and spokes principle. Packages would be collected and driven along truck routes (the spokes) and driven to hub airports where a waiting airplane would take them to a central location—Memphis would be ideal—where they would be sorted and put aboard planes to their final destination.

An "Impractical" Idea

Smith's professor told him the idea was interesting and well formed but impractical. It would never work. And since part of the assignment was to come up with a practical and feasible idea, his grade would be adjusted accordingly. He got a "C" on the paper.

After he graduated from college, Smith joined the Marine Corps and went to Vietnam because he thought it was his patriotic duty. He served two tours of duty and won six medals for bravery, including a Silver Star and two Purple Hearts. Vietnam changed Smith, but not in the way it disenchanted many young American soldiers. In their book, *Breakthroughs!*, P. Ranganath Nayak and John M. Ketteringham say that Smith was not only distressed about the lives he saw wasted in sudden death, but he was also discouraged by the lives he saw that would be wasted in the future because the "managerial class" who hired these workingmen would expect so little from them—and get it.[1]

Treating Others with Respect

Smith learned that powerless people demand only one thing from life and their fellowman, and that one thing is respect. When you have nothing else, respect becomes all important.

---

[1]P. Ranganath Nayak, Ph.D., and John M. Ketteringham, Ph.D., *Breakthroughs!* (New York: Rawson Associates, 1986), 318–319.

When people are treated with respect, they respond with fierce loyalty and dedication. They give their hearts and souls to leaders who treat them as they deserve to be treated.

As a young officer, Smith also learned in Vietnam that the only imperative of leadership is to take care of your men. The only goal in war or peace, he believed, should be to get all your people to a better place, a safer place, from where they are now. A good leader would not lead people into danger unless he or she was convinced that they could be led out into safety. Smith saw firsthand that ordinary people performed incredible feats when they were asked to do so, when their leaders believed in them and trusted them. That concept became Smith's passion in life and the founding principle of Federal Express.

It wasn't easy. For Smith's hub and spokes plan to work, he would have to provide national service on the first day of operation, an approach that would require enormous capital. He couldn't start small and work his way up. To buy the necessary airplanes and equipment, he invested all of his own money and borrowed from family, friends, and banks. For most of the company's early years, it teetered on the verge of bankruptcy. His own family sued him and he was prosecuted for fraud. The suit was dropped, and he was found innocent of the fraud charges, but the pressures were enormous.

On the first day of operation as a national air freight service, Federal Express delivered a grand total of *six* packages. On occasion, employees were asked not to cash their paychecks because the company didn't have enough money in the bank to cover them. Despite his personal difficulties and those of the company, however, Smith never compromised on his loyalty to his employees.

Sharing the Risk

"Foreclosure was a reality that threatened everybody, the boss as well as the working stiff," Nayak and Ketteringham found, "and when everybody had to deal with it, it didn't seem so awful. As Tucker Taylor, an aviator in the used plane business that Smith retained to study the feasibility of the Federal Express idea, pointed out, everybody at Federal was an entrepreneur; one man's idea about starting a new office in a strange place was as good as anybody else's. 'For the first three years, we didn't know what we were doing,' said Taylor. 'Really. Literally. We didn't have any data about the market. So when you opened a station in Miami, you found the best kid you could, you gave him a map of Miami, and told him to call you if he had any problems.' "

Couriers were pretty much left on their own to figure out how to pick up the packages and get them to the airport on time. There were no layers of management to supervise their every move, and nobody really cared how they got the job done, only that it *was* done. Stories made the rounds in the company about drivers who were so committed to the company that they hocked their watches to buy gasoline to operate their vehicles.

Smith repaid their devotion in kind. Regardless of how bad things were, the company stuck together, just as his platoon had in Vietnam. There were no layoffs. Ever. Workers might be shifted around; pilots became station managers until there was enough business to get them back on the flight line again, but they didn't lose their jobs.

Empowered Employees

Fred Smith empowered his employees long before it became a fashionable trend in business. He and they went on to build one of the world's greatest success stories. We didn't even know we needed overnight delivery service until Smith made it possible. In less than twenty years, Federal Express built—from nothing—a $7.7 billion company with eighty-five thousand employees worldwide. In 1990, Federal Express became the eighth company ever—and the first service company—to receive the Malcolm Baldridge National Quality Award, the country's most prestigious award for quality.

The strict criteria for the award include considerable emphasis on the way a company treats its employees and the way they treat their customers. From its early days, Federal Express surveyed its customers to find out what they liked or didn't like about the company, and the questionnaires would come back with little notes inscribed upon them with a personal message about one courier or another. Federal Express realized early on that customers did business with its people, not with the corporation.

Arthur Bass, another of Smith's early recruits, recalled "the number of people who called me during the early days to say, 'We think your company is just as screwed-up as (the competition). I wanted to tell you that because I don't have the heart to tell your courier, because that kid is busting his ass out here for you, and we are going to be sure that you still get the packages. But if you ever screw up again, that's going to be it.' The kids had built this unbelievable feeling in the company."[2]

The "Federal Feeling"

In an enthusiastic telephone interview, Jean Ward-Jones, manager of quality education and administration, told me how the feeling still persists in the company today. Federal Express has flipped the typical pyramidal structure on its head, she says. "Our customers are at the top, and immediately next to our customers are our employees. Then the full hierarchy of management is turned upside down to ensure that they recognize their only function is to serve their employees and enable their employees to serve their customers better."

The company's philosophy encompasses three elements: people, service, and profit. In its literature, Federal Express explains the philosophy: "Our company always balances the needs of employees, our customers, and our shareholders, considering each in making plans or policies. We always consider the effects on our people first in making decisions, recognizing that if we take care of our employees, they will deliver a superior service which our customers will, in turn, utilize. Only by making a surplus of profit can we ensure our company's continued existence, future opportunities, and our employment."

To ensure that the "Federal feeling" would continue as the company grew, Federal Express established policies that would institutionalize the respect for individual performance

---

[2]Nayak and Ketteringham, 334.

upon which Smith founded the company. Managers are required to complete performance reviews twice a year, and they are trained extensively in the process so they know how to evaluate their employees effectively in order to help them to grow and develop. A bimonthly report advises managers which employees are due for a performance review.

Another report lists employees who didn't receive performance reviews on time. "This is one of the most seriously studied reports in the company," Ward-Jones says. "If managers are not conducting performance reviews on time, it is sending a message to employees that they are not very important, and that's very serious. One of the worst things a manager can do is get behind in performance reviews. You just don't do that.

"There should be no surprises in a performance review. Instead, there should be daily input so that when the employee gets the formal review, it is exactly as he or she thought it would be. There should be no big gaps between how the employee thinks he is performing and how the manager thinks he is performing. That shouldn't happen," Ward-Jones says.

Turning the Tables on Management

In March of each year, the tables are turned, and employees have the opportunity to evaluate their management. Questionnaires are transmitted to employees by computer and answered the same way. Every employee can express his views of his immediate manager and all the levels above, the specifics of employee benefit programs, and the company as a whole. To provide continuity, employees are asked if issues they raised in the previous year's evaluation were handled to their satisfaction.

Responses are anonymous, but a summary of responses from direct reports is provided to every manager. Employees rate their managers on specific leadership attributes, which are then analyzed to identify any changes the manager needs to make. Employees are encouraged to facilitate two-way communication and help their managers focus on the specific attributes that most require their attention.

The management evaluation process is balanced against specific, measurable people, service, and profit goals to keep it from degenerating into a popularity contest. And, in the spirit of continuous improvement, every person is expected to show gains over the previous year.

Measuring Customer Satisfaction Daily

Customer satisfaction measures are even more stringent. Performance against twelve specific criteria (late, lost or damaged packages, delays in answering phone calls, etc.) are measured daily. Measurements are weighted according to the severity of the problem—failure to pick up a package or damaging a package are considered the worst failures—to produce an index the company calls its Service Quality Indicator. The SQI is the company's precise measure of how well it meets its customers' expectations. In staff functions where the SQI measurement system may not directly apply, managers are expected to develop their own service quality indicators.

The combination of SQI measurements, employee performance reviews, and management evaluations help synchronize corporate and individual goals. Quarterly and annual individual goals should support the company's overall people, service, and profit goals. Individual bonuses depend upon the entire corporation's meeting its people, service, and profit objectives.

''That's how we keep this from turning into a popularity contest,'' says Ward-Jones. ''If I am so lax on my employees that I will let them do whatever so that they will give me good scores, then in all likelihood, I am not going to meet my service requirements, because I haven't made them responsible for meeting their stretch goals. I haven't enabled them to develop, I haven't forced hard decisions, and I probably haven't been as tough as I needed to be. If, on the other hand, I come down so hard that I don't meet any of my management evaluation goals, but meet all of my service goals, then I have gone too far. The system keeps me in balance.''

What's in It for Me?

Part of the FedEx culture is that every employee has the right to ask, ''What's in it for me?'' They are not expected to follow blindly along simply because someone tells them to do so. And, if they don't believe they have been treated fairly by the system, they may seek redress through a grievance process called the "guaranteed fair treatment" procedure. If they think they deserved a promotion that they didn't get or if they believe their performance evaluations were unfair, they may file a grievance.

If the employee's director cannot work out a satisfactory solution to the problem, it goes to a vice president. If it still remains in dispute, the last stop is a board of appeals which Ward-Jones describes as "similar to a trial." The employee and the manager may each present three "witnesses" to present information and speak on their behalf. The board of appeals then makes the final decision. "When they go to this board, all the information is going to be heard," Ward-Jones says. "The people in this company truly believe that if they have an issue, it will be heard and it will be resolved fairly."

Being a manager at Federal Express is not an easy task, a fact that is made known early on to those who express an interest in advancement to the management ranks. Prospective managers are required to complete a leadership effective awareness program (LEAP) that combines intensive, focused study with on-the-job management training. If they demonstrate management potential, the first step is completion of the course curriculum. If they show they can cut it, prospective managers must then find a sponsor who is willing to spend several months training them on the job.

During this six- to nine-month training period, trainees gradually assume more and more management responsibilities. When they have completed the program and their sponsoring manager thinks they are ready, one step remains. They must receive a final endorsement from a panel of managers that interviews them at length to determine their suitability for a management job. Most managers are developed this way— from within. In fact, the company says that less than thirty percent of *all* new employees come from the outside.

Bravo Zulu Awards

Federal Express motivates workers in a variety of other ways. When someone does something that his or her manager considers above and beyond the call of duty, he or she may receive a "Bravo Zulu" award. BZs, as they are called, like many other characteristics of the company, are based on

Smith's background as a Marine Corps aviator. BZ is the semaphore signal from the aircraft carrier to the pilot congratulating him on a good landing. It's a ''well done,'' an ''attaboy,'' in Marine Corps parlance.

FedEx managers are given sheets of BZ decals that they may affix to notes or letters sent to their employees. ''Employees know it's a special thing,'' says Ward-Jones. ''It's a little bit more than just saying it was good. You wouldn't believe as you walk around here how many Bravo Zulus are posted in the cubicles. It's like we have a currency of BZs.''

For performance that exceeds a typical BZ, managers may request a $25 or $50 check that they can send to a worker who just performed an exceptional task. It is accompanied by a BZ certificate—with the Bravo Zulu semaphore flags in the center—and a description of the outstanding activity. It's an immediate payback for exceptional performance, and it is not charged to the manager's budget. The manager makes the decision whether or not to award the cash and certificate based solely on merit.

Superstar Program

Those who consistently outperform their peers may regularly see the fruits of their efforts in their paycheck. At performance evaluation time, managers may submit superior achievers' names for inclusion in the company's ''Superstar'' program. Those who make it into this elite group can expect to receive up to ten percent more in their paycheck, based on their exceptional performance.

Fred Smith seems to have found a way to institutionalize in Federal Express his basic values by incorporating respect in a variety of innovative management and employee motivation programs. Empowered employees know they have the full resources of the company behind them, and that they are responsible for their own destinies. How they perform is entirely up to them.

Smith learned from his days in the Marine Corps the basic tenets of leadership that continue to evade many CEOs: Today's employees are not stupid. They know very well what's going on in the company and they can quickly determine the difference between a boss who really cares about their welfare and one who wants them to do more with less for his own selfish reasons.

Perception Gaps

Many managers are, in fact, so out of touch that they can't even relate to the people who work for them. Louis Harris & Associates found what they called a ''perception gap'' between what the employees wanted and what management thought they wanted when they surveyed the office workers and their managers a few years ago.

Reporting on the ''Trust Gap'' in *Fortune*, writer Alan Farnham said: ''Managers assume, for instance, that job security is of paramount importance to employees. In fact, among workers it ranks far below such ethereal-sounding desires as respect, a higher standard of management ethics, increased recognition of employee contributions, and closer, more honest communications between employees and senior management.''[3]

Farnham found that when executives start talking about teamwork, trust, and employee empowerment, they had better be ready to back it up with action. It isn't enough for the CEO to hold a meeting and give a speech about how ''we're all in this together,'' and continue to treat hourly workers as second-class citizens incapable of thinking or keeping up with what's going on in the company.

Actions That Demonstrate Mutual Caring and Support

According to *Fortune*, there are several simple actions that any company can implement to begin to develop an atmosphere of mutual caring and support among the bosses and the workers:

1. Make the pay more equitable in order to link the financial interests of the top and the bottom. Link compensation to performance over which beneficiaries have control, and

---

[3]Alan Farnham, ''The Trust Gap,'' *Fortune* (December 4, 1989), 56+.

redistribute the exposure to risk and reward.

2. Rethink perks. Since executives now have to pay tax on them anyway, they don't mean as much as they once did, and they still have the same downside with the rank and file. Instead, pay them in cash and keep them focused on the business instead of competing for the corner office or the Oriental rug.

3. Make the office layout more equitable. Show all the people you care about them instead of demonstrating to them by the size of their office that they are second-class citizens.

4. Communicate. Make sure your door really is open and employees know they can talk to you about the things that bother them.

5. Survey employee attitudes. Ask them what they think to get them involved in shaping the place where they work. People are reasonable and they know they can't have everything they want. Just make sure their views are considered.

6. Have face-to-face meetings to explain things, no matter how difficult the subject. Go to the cafeteria and talk to employees once in awhile. Sit with them and drink coffee out of Styrofoam cups.

7. Be open and honest with employees. Play it straight with them and don't withhold bad news until the last minute. If you are going to close a plant, tell them as far in advance as possible to allow them to adjust their lives accordingly.

8. Respect them. If you are generous with them, they will respond in kind.

9. Put yourself in their shoes once in awhile. McDonald's sends its executives out to cook hamburgers, Hyatt Hotels sent its headquarters staff out to work as elevator operators, maids, waiters, and doormen. It gives you a better appreciation for what employees do, and they respect you for it.

10. Don't be afraid to be hokey. Send birthday cards to employees or throw a party where the executives serve the workers, but make sure you are sincere. Hokey things are meaningless unless they are accompanied by honest com-

munication, respectful treatment, and equitable standards
of gain and sacrifice.

Key Points and Action Items

1. Trust is not something that can be created with words alone. It must be backed up with action. If you show others that you trust them, they are far more likely to live up to your expectations.

2. Evaluate the alternatives. Which is worse: doubting others and creating friction between you or trusting them to do their jobs and allowing them to deal with the consequences if they fail?

3. As Fred Smith at Federal Express found, ordinary people will do extraordinary things if you believe in them, support them, and simply allow them to excel.

4. The only imperative of leadership is to take care of your people. Do not lead them into something from which there is no escape. Take care of your people and they will take care of you—and your customers.

5. Follow the Golden Rule in your dealings with others. If you simply treat others as you would like to be treated, they will reward you with loyalty and devotion. Give them the respect they deserve.

16

Your Anchor

*Faith is the substance of things hoped for,
the evidence of things not seen.*

—Hebrews 11:1

Forty-four miles northwest of Donald Trump's Plaza Hotel in midtown Manhattan, nestled in the foothills of the Ramapo Mountains, lies the little town of Ringwood, New Jersey, population fourteen thousand. The landscape is dotted with lakes and the forests are protected from land developers by the foresight of the town's founder. When he died, he donated fifteen thousand acres of the surrounding land to the state to preserve the beauty of the region.

The town was founded around 1740 when the mountains were found to contain rich iron ore. Ringwood's iron was used in every major war from the French and Indian War through the Korean conflict. (The mines closed in 1957.) Legend has it that George Washington visited Ringwood several times to inspect the manufacture of cannonballs during the Revolutionary War, and Ringwood Manor—a state park that was once the estate of the mines' proprietor—is the final resting place of one of the two remaining cannons from "Old Ironsides."

It is a bedroom community that is home to commuters who can't afford to—or choose not to—live in more upscale Bergen County next door. It is also home to the Jackson Whites, a racially mixed community of blacks and whites who worked together, lived together, and intermarried as they worked the mines.

The town is bisected by the only feeder road into the highways leading into New York. On a clear day, drivers may catch a glimpse of Manhattan's magnificent skyline from the top of the mountain, a fact that no doubt led to its being named "Skyline Drive." By 7:00 A.M. every weekday, the traffic is bumper-to-bumper from the center of Ringwood to the toll gates of the George Washington Bridge into upper Manhattan, jammed with commuters who fervently believe they have the best of both worlds—living in the country and working in the city.

Ministering to the Spiritually Needy

It is the job of Reverend Benhardt Fraumann, pastor of the Community Presbyterian Church of Ringwood, to minister to a few hundred of the spiritually needy who live there. Known simply as "Ben" to his flock, no one could be better suited to the job of guiding a bunch of iconoclasts than Fraumann.

In the introduction to the church's membership directory, he writes: "If you are looking for the perfect church . . . you will not find it here at the Community Presbyterian Church of Ringwood. On the other hand, if you do find the perfect church, by all means don't join it . . . your presence will undoubtedly wreck it . . . and there ought to be one somewhere.

"We know that we are incredibly imperfect, but that God loves and uses us anyway and that the heavenly host applauds any stumble in the right direction. This belief is freeing. And we attempt to let everybody also be free in their practice of the faith. Christ will meet us where we are in our life journey. We must all grow at our own speed and every individual must live out his or her own relationship in work and grace.

Celebrating Theological Diversity

"Therefore we do not tolerate theological diversity here, we affirm it. We are attempting to discover Grace as a way of life. 'Now there are varieties of gifts, but the same Spirit; and there are varieties of service, but the same Lord.'

"And, finally, we attempt to be led by joy. Life is hard. Tragedy comes on its own terms and we deal with it then. We believe that the most important character trait a Christian can possess is to be an instrument of joy."

Before you walk through the portals of the church, you know it is going to be an interesting experience. You won't find canned sermons at Ringwood Presbyterian, adapted from a collection of the world's finest sermons. Fraumann's sermons are real, often earthy, and uplifting. To entice newcomers to make an initial visit, he offers to preach on any topic they choose—and he lives up to the promise. When our dog died, he delivered a eulogy for "Jack" and a sermon designed to help children—and their parents—learn to cope with the death of a loved one, animal or human. Jack would have been proud.

Fraumann's ministerial appeal transcends the narrow tenets of a denomination to reach out to a broad audience. He has the grace of a confident Christian, the soul of a philosopher, and the charisma of a television preacher. He's turned down many offers to move to larger, more affluent churches—including a huge congregation in New York—convinced that he is right where he belongs.

A Youthful Search

Although he doesn't attach much importance to his youthful rebellion, it is precisely his own experience in finding the importance of spirituality in life that has allowed him to relate to others who are having trouble finding the way. Because of his own past, he can empathize in a way that would be impossible for someone who had not traveled a similar path.

Recently, Fraumann and his wife, Nora, interrupted a visit with their parents to spend a pleasant summer afternoon with Merrilee and me. As we talked of the great mysteries of life, Fraumann recalled for us his involvement in the church and how he came to be a minister.

Raised in a Christian home in suburban Detroit where his father was an active member of the church, Fraumann loved going to church as a child. "I was always impressed with the majesty of the worship of God," he says. "The music, and in some ways the austerity of it, just resonated with my soul. I was impressed as a boy that this was where adults went, and I was impressed with the absolute laws of God. I didn't question them. I accepted them as fact.

"As a boy, my grandfather who lived with us read the Bible to me. I vividly recall one of those experiences. I was about eight years old when he read to me the story of the crucifixion, and he began to cry. I was astonished. Grandfathers don't cry! So I assumed that this must be very important, even though it was something I didn't fully understand.

"When I was fourteen, I went to debate camp—I planned to be a lawyer or a politician—and there I met two high school seniors who were going to enter the ministry. Until then, I had never considered the possibility. I remember praying about it and saying that if God would accept my service I would do it—so long as he didn't send me to Africa or someplace like that. I thought about it off and on through high school, but never really made a serious commitment."

In 1967, Fraumann enrolled in the journalism school at Northwestern University. There he charged headlong into the sixties, rebelling with a vengeance against his strict Protestant upbringing. He embraced the flower power counterculture, but never really became part of it. He considered himself a journalist, more of a dispassionate observer of the movement than a part of it. Eventually, like many of his contemporaries, he dropped out. He wanted to travel Europe and write the great American novel.

More Lost than Ever

Nothing really helped him "find himself"; instead, he was more lost than ever. Finally, he returned to school, graduated from the University of Michigan and entered the seminary to honor the pledge to enter the ministry that he had made almost a decade earlier. The problem was that the seminary was not as he expected it to be. Instead of engaging in constant prayer and meditation, it was an academic exercise in studying contradictory axioms, in an attempt to apply a Western scientific view to the Bible.

Fraumann struggled to gain understanding, particularly with the resurrection of Christ, which he knew was key to the faith. "I prayed, but I couldn't ever figure out what the resurrection was. Everybody kept telling me that it was the foundation of Christianity, but I couldn't get there. It either happened or it didn't, but intellectually I couldn't reconcile it with everything else I knew about life and death.''

A Seminal Experience

The turning point in Fraumann's life came in the summer of his first year of seminary when he served as chaplain of a hospital in West Virginia that cared for black lung patients. He was touched by the courage of good men who labored at backbreaking jobs to care for their families—and died from it—and he was troubled by their anger at God. They raged and they asked the big question: ''If God is good and has so much power, why is there so much suffering? You tell me that God is good, yet I just read that there was a tidal wave in Bangladesh that killed a few thousand people. Please reconcile those two facts for me.''

At twenty-three years of age, Fraumann was still struggling with his own beliefs, and he was ill-equipped to deal with the suffering and death he encountered among the poor coal miners of West Virginia. Alone and lonely, during his first night on the job, he was asked to comfort the families of five who died in the hospital and to counsel a mother who had allowed her five-year-old child to starve to death. ''This is a tough business when you're twenty-three and frankly haven't got your own head on straight,'' he recalls.

One particularly lonely night he was called to the bedside of an eighty-seven-year-old woman who was dying. ''In many respects I was still a fuzzy-headed liberal and in some respects I still believed in a muscular type of Christianity, the kind that sends you out to go to college, get a law degree, and change the world. But this woman was going to do none of those things. She was going to die in that bed. In about a month. Painfully. I asked myself: 'What do I—a pseudo optimistic liberal—have to offer this woman?'

The Presence of God

''She asked me to pray with her, and I can truly say this was the major religious experience of my life. In the midst of that prayer, I felt the overwhelming presence of God. I don't go around hearing voices in my head, but at that moment, I heard the voice of God. I heard the voice of Christ saying, 'This is why I died. I died for this woman.'

"The experience blew me away. I have never since been the same. Suddenly, Christianity made sense to me—the meaning of the cross and the resurrection were clear to me. For the first time it struck me: you can go to law school and change the world, but there comes a time when you die. At that moment the kind of life you've lived and the kind of person you have chosen to be are between you and God—and no one else. Without God, we are all alone in death.

"I have had other deep religious experiences since, but they were not a watershed event like the one I experienced that night. I had a lot of work and a lot of learning to do—and I still do—but the point is it came from the outside. It came from God. For me, it was a Eureka! experience, a moment of great discovery."

A Changed Man

Fraumann emerged from the experience a changed man, one with a meaning and purpose. He reevaluated his life and re-thought his entire value system. He read voraciously to understand so he could explain. His knowledge and understanding allow him to place Christianity in the context of history and philosophy and to explain it convincingly to the most devout skeptic. His is a brand of religion that is deep; it is personal and it is lasting. It is one that is destined to last and to change the lives of many.

Since his West Virginia experience, he has helped many others deal with crises in their lives—marriage or financial problems, illness, and a death in the family—and he says without exception, such events change our lives forever. Some people respond to crisis with strength and become better people for having gone through it, and some fall apart, but all are changed.

Such times in our lives have the effect of focusing our attention totally and completely upon the things that really matter: life, health, love, the importance of family and friends —and the power of faith. It is often during a personal crisis that we turn to God for help, but the important thing to remember, Fraumann says, is that God *always* loves us whether or not we are willing to accept or acknowledge it. He is always there for us. Crises come and go throughout our lives—they are a part of life—but God's love is forever.

A Muslim's Pilgrimage

Another whose moment of truth came with a dramatic revelation was Khalil "Chuck" Alawan, chairman of the board of the Islamic Center of Detroit, the largest mosque in North America. I read about Alawan in the newspaper and was impressed with his attempts to help young Muslims reconcile their religious beliefs with western society. I phoned him, described this book, and asked him if he would be willing to be interviewed for it. He graciously accepted and we agreed to meet for breakfast at a diner roughly halfway between our homes.

Our rapport was instantaneous, facilitated by a garrulous food server and our dietary restrictions (his religious, mine self-inflicted). In the industrial strength cholesterol environment in which we found ourselves, our food choices and the topic of our conversation greatly amused our waitress. The tape recording of the interview is punctuated with her observations about our skimpy breakfast and the "pretty heavy conversation" in which we were engaged.

A devout Shiite Muslim whose family immigrated to this country from Lebanon, there was never a doubt in Alawan's mind that he would fulfill the requirement of his faith to make the trek through Saudi Arabia in summer to visit the holy shrines of Mecca and Medina. For a Muslim, the pilgrimage to Mecca is more than a Catholic's visit to the Vatican or a Jew's journey to Jerusalem. It is a requirement of the faith, spelled out in the Koran.

"I was mentally and spiritually prepared for the trip," Alawan says. "It was an in-between time for me at work and I had the time. I have always been a Muslim, but not always a good one. I strayed from my community for a while because I was a hypocrite. I drank alcohol, and never really got into the faith. I sort of stayed on the perimeters. I wasn't practicing the things I would be preaching, the things that are taught in the Koran. The point at which a person fully accepts Islam is an individual thing," Alawan says. "Eventually the day comes when every Muslim comes face-to-face with it.

"For me, the trip to Mecca was like being born again. What it meant to me was that I got a second chance to apply my faith. I think my transformation was going on earlier, but this was the thing that brought it to a head. All my life, I have been convinced that there is a Creator, but the Muslim has been spared a physical vision of God. We are told that we do not have the senses to even visualize the Creator. For us, it is a tremendous, indescribable, knowing force. We know that we can't understand it, so we just accept it as fact. We are no different than any other human beings in terms of sophistication. We know the scientific development of the world; we know about the environment. We are told things in the Koran that—given the fact they were written fifteen to sixteen hundred years ago—are pretty sophisticated about creation.

Finding a Special Path

"I had the Koran to guide me, and I have always believed that it was the word of God as given to Mohammed. My religion was reinforced because I couldn't deny the fact that Mohammed existed, and I could not deny him the right to be considered truthful. So, I had to accept as fact that the Koran was the revelation of God. Somewhere in my mid to late forties"—Alawan is sixty-two today—"I became quite cognizant that there was this greater force, and that even though I wasn't a chosen one, there was a special path for me. All I had to do was identify it.

"It wasn't really a fact of my upbringing as much as it was the result of my own search. I really studied other faiths, and I became convinced that, in fact, Muslims are nothing more than an extension of Christianity. There is only one Creator, only one true belief, and that it is all nothing more than the revelation that a Creator existed. He had people on earth that he communicated with—and not just the five major prophets. Islam believes that all religions come from the same source; they differ only because of human frailties. The message given at the source was consistent throughout the time of the revelation."

Islam in Western Society

Alawan says it was against this backdrop, "I was trying to get to me. I was trying very hard to take Islam and apply it to the society we live in. It is difficult. It is hard in Western society to stop whatever we are doing, wash our face, hands, arms, and feet (because those are the points that touch the prayer rug, the symbol of a pure place), prostrate ourselves, and pray five times a day. It is difficult not to eat pork or any other animal flesh that has not been slaughtered purposely for food, and a prayer offered at the time. In our society, it is very difficult to have opinions on abortion, drinking of alcohol, taking drugs, and homosexuality that are very terse. Islam is very difficult to understand by much of our society. What we are is a people trying to follow our faith in a society that in many ways is hostile."

In 1984, Alawan made his personal pilgrimage to Mecca. He flew to Medina in search of the "oneness with God" that his father described during his own pilgrimage in 1948. In Medina, Alawan exchanged his western clothing for a simple gown and he joined the faithful from all over the world as they visited the holy shrines and spent an afternoon in prayer out in the desert.

It was at a small mosque located between Medina and Mecca that the prophet Mohammed frequented, that Alawan completed his connection with Islam. The place was important to him not only because of its religious significance, but also because his father had often told him of a spiritual renewal that he had experienced at that exact spot.

Finding the True Meaning

As he stood on that sacred ground, Alawan felt overwhelmed. Stripped of everything worldly, everything that had caused problems for him in the past was removed. He felt cleansed from the ills of the world and safe from harm. He also felt the overwhelming presence of God and of his dead father. At that moment, he understood the true meaning of Islam, and he accepted it fully.

Today, Alawan is a partner and vice president of sales at Altair Industries, a firm located in Brighton, Michigan (near

Detroit), that fabricates metal walls and other products for industrial buildings. Despite the demands of the business, he finds the time not only to practice his own faith, but also to help others "fit the square peg of Islam into the round hole of western culture." It is because of his own experience that he has been able to "make Islam user-friendly" for Muslims—particularly young people—in America.

It hasn't been easy. Most Americans' view of Islam is based on images of Arab oil cartels, Ayatollah Khomeini's revolution in Iran, hostage-taking in Lebanon and the World Trade Center bombing. He tries to help young Muslims practice their faith amid the distrust they often encounter. "A lot of the older people look at certain subject matters as things they should avoid," Allie Souweidane, a thirty-two year old Muslim whose parents emigrated to the U.S. from Lebanon, told the *Detroit News and Free Press*. "Chuck is not the type of person to do that. He forces them to look directly at a situation and confront it head on."[1]

Alawan regularly preaches to and counsels teenagers at the Islamic Center mosque and he serves as an adviser on Islamic issues to the regional Boy Scout council. He is also an active member of the Detroit Interfaith Roundtable, a group that attempts to improve relations among Christians, Jews, and Muslims.

A Constant Struggle

"We don't have an easy time here in the U.S.," Alawan says. "My mind is more eastern than it is western. Christianity is an eastern religion, but it has been westernized. That hasn't taken place with Islam. Because Islam began some six hundred years after Jesus, it is fully recorded and documented, and it handsomely interprets the life of the prophet. The flavor is there; the images are there. We like our Islamic culture. We enjoy it; we want to follow it; we preach it, and we want to apply it, but it is pretty hard to make that round peg fit into the square hole.

"So we have to struggle. The Islamic word for struggle is

---

[1]Christopher Cook, "Businessman's Life Shows How Islam Is User-friendly," *Detroit News and Free Press*, Saturday, 4 July 1992, 1A, 7A.

jihad, but the west has interpreted the word to mean a call to war—bring out your swords. But the greatest jihad is the internal struggle, the struggle within. That struggle is probably the best way to explain my existence here. I'm as American as apple pie. I've served my country, and I love my flag, but there is an element of my being that relates to the Islamic culture. It goes on in my business and social life.

"The very essence of being alive is so that you can struggle. To a Muslim, the devil, as he is called in Christianity, is very real. We call him 'the whisperer.' You may think of him as your alter ego, the little voice that tempts you. I believe the more you live on the straight path in all aspects of your life, the more he whispers. You are not acceptable to him, so he tries to tempt you to stray from the path. That's part of the struggle.

"Happily, there is also a Creator. For me, he is as real as my own image that I see in the mirror. It is not something that I believe simply because I'm afraid not to believe. The simplest statement in science is that you cannot destroy matter. You can change its form, but it cannot be destroyed. Human beings cannot be destroyed. The physical body can be destroyed, but not the human being. That fact alone attests to me that there is a Creator and everything I do on earth is, as I am taught to do, in conjunction with the Creator. He has promised me that there is no end, only an end to the physical form, not to the ultimate goal. Because I believe that, my faith is a very viable, very important part of my life."

Alawan believes that we must condition ourselves to receive the benefit of spirituality. He likens it to a safecracker sanding his fingertips to heighten his sense of touch in order to feel the tumblers of the lock fall into place as he attempts to crack the combination. Only by honing our spiritual senses can we prepare ourselves to receive the message. "That is what I am trying to do with my life," Alawan says.

The Importance of Spirituality

In conducting research for this and other self-help books, I have been amazed at the number of people who—when they have been convinced that I am truly interested in learning in order to convey useful information to others—have told me similar stories of self-discovery. They may not be as dramatic as Fraumann's or Alawan's, but they were deep, personal experiences that changed their lives.

I have a generous portion of the journalistic cynicism and skepticism that Fraumann described, but I am convinced that a book about success would not be complete without a reference to spirituality. Since I've made it a point to ask, virtually every successful person I've interviewed has told me of the importance of religion in his or her life.

It's been my good fortune over the years to conduct seminars on motivation and achievement for a number of corporations, trade associations, professional societies, and other organizations, and I always include a mention of the importance of spirituality in achieving success. I tell them that it doesn't matter if it is Judaism, Christianity, Islam, Zen-Buddhism, Psychokinesis, or the Great Cosmic Consciousness, it is old as history itself to believe in something larger than ourselves. The important thing is that unless we are anchored to a belief that encompasses more than ourselves and our small circle, much of the true meaning of life is lost. Without some degree of spirituality, the attainment of the full measure of success is impossible. It is an essential ingredient of a truly balanced life.

Without exception, after those sessions someone always tells me: "I'm glad you included something about spirituality. It's an important part of my life and, I suspect, just about everyone else's, but most of the time we don't talk about it in a business setting. I'm glad you brought it up."

When I worked on the book *Believe and Achieve* with W. Clement Stone, he invited me to breakfast at his home in suburban Chicago, a magnificent villa overlooking Lake Michigan. When we sat down at the long dining table adorned with a spun gold tablecloth, as the servants stood quietly in the background, he bowed his head to say grace, and to thank God for his many blessings. Religion is an important part of his life and he celebrates his faith in everything he does.

Many Roads to the Center

It would be impossible, of course, in a single chapter of a book to pay tribute to the effect of all the great religions upon civilization. My own life has been positively influenced by ministers, friends, and mentors of a great variety of religious beliefs: Jewish, Muslim, Catholic, a variety of Protestants, Mormons, and others. I have learned from them all equally, and I am more convinced than ever that spirituality in some form is an innate part of mankind, as essential as the breath of life itself. Despite the apparent differences between faiths, we are all seeking the same thing, and notwithstanding many opinions to the contrary, I believe there many roads to the center. The one you select is up to you.

I chose to profile Ben Fraumann and Chuck Alawan in this chapter because I believe they both have the noble quality of tolerance, an understanding and respect for others that encourages and celebrates diversity of belief, while they are confident and serene in the knowledge that they are on the right course themselves. They help point the way to anyone who cares to travel with them, but they respect others who have chosen a different path. They are making a difference in a world disenchanted by traditional religious beliefs.

In the end, the quest for a state of faith that allows one to accept religion as an important part of a balanced life is the ultimate personal decision. There may be a single answer, there may be no right answer, or there may be any number of right answers, but one thing is certain: We will most certainly become better people for having undertaken the search.

Key Points and Action Items

1. As Reverend Ben Fraumann noted, we are not perfect, but God loves us despite our imperfections. We must all develop spiritually at our own speed and work out our own beliefs.

2. There comes a time when you die. At that moment, the kind of person you have chosen to become is between you and God, and no one else. Without God, we are all alone in death.

3. In his quest to make Islam "user-friendly," Chuck Alawan has proved that it is possible to practice your faith in an inhospitable environment. It only requires determination and dedication.

4. You must give before you can receive. Like a safe-cracker sanding his fingertips to heighten his sense of touch, we must condition ourselves in order to receive the benefit of spirituality.

5. Spirituality is an important component of success and of life. The path you select is not nearly as important as making a commitment to choose the right path for you. There are many roads to the center. Your choice is yours alone.

17

A Creative Life

*Life is what happens to you
while you are busy making other plans.*

—John Lennon

"You want to know how to make a small fortune? Start off with a large one and go into the airline business."

The speaker is Richard Branson, the puckish British billionaire, adventurer, world-record holder, founder and majority owner of Virgin Airways. The setting is New York's trendy Arcadia restaurant. Branson's staff has reserved the entire restaurant to host a luncheon for travel writers to introduce a new frequent flyer program. Journalists who have packed the restaurant for the occasion laugh appreciatively at Branson's joke.

In his casual clothes—he seldom wears a tie and usually travels only with his ubiquitous black notebook and passport—and closely clipped beard he looks more like a down-on-his-luck writer than the chairman and chief executive officer of a $1.3 billion travel and entertainment conglomerate. He makes several attempts to read a prepared speech, banters with the audience, laments that he's no good at reading speeches, and finally parodies his own speech in a singsong voice. The audience loves it.

Branson's arrival is something of an occasion. He has been

driven to the restaurant in a horse-drawn carriage; the driver is wearing a "Fly Virgin" T-shirt and the horse is sporting a matching cap. Branson, holding a giant carrot symbolizing the incentives Virgin hopes will attract frequent flyers, climbs aboard the horse to pose for photos. Cameras click and motorized film advances buzz as photographers record the event staged for their benefit.

An "Adventure Capitalist"

The head of England's third-largest privately owned company is unconcerned when the horse beneath him begins to kick and buck in defiance of his unwanted passenger. He hangs on expertly, patting the horse to calm him, smiling broadly all the while. This is pretty tame stuff for a self-styled "adventure capitalist" who has crossed the Atlantic Ocean twice in a speedboat and both the Atlantic and the Pacific in a hot air balloon, a man whose chief requirements in life are met, according to *Vanity Fair*, "whenever a great force of will can be set against singularly bad odds."[1]

A sometimes shy, always fun-loving prankster, Branson has made a fortune doing what others thought couldn't be done, and his exploits of derring-do, some for promotional purposes and some purely for the fun of it, have become legend. He's water skied behind a blimp, parachuted from airplanes, and was delivered to his own wedding dangling from the landing struts of a helicopter.

Britain's premier entrepreneur—British students recently rated him the third most admired man in the world (behind the pope and the Prince of Wales)—demonstrated his knack for capitalizing on his business sense, wit, and keen sense of humor at an early age. When he dropped out of public school, his headmaster predicted: "You will either go to prison or become a millionaire." He almost did both.

Publisher at Eighteen

His first venture was the launch of a magazine in 1968, which he called *Student*. He raised the money to publish the

---

[1]Fred Goodman, "The Virgin King," *Vanity Fair* (May 1992), 172.

first issue by selling $10,000 in advertising over the phone, telling potential advertisers that he was eighteen years old and publishing a magazine that was doing something "really useful" for young people. The upstart magazine garnered a good deal of publicity for Branson, largely because of his ability to persuade British celebrities to write for it.

The inaugural issue of *Student* included interviews with Vanessa Redgrave and several other British personalities of the day, and a short story donated to the magazine by John le Carré. Branson had secured their cooperation simply by asking. He discovered that famous people were willing to help if he merely wrote to them and requested an interview.

The Record Business

Despite its high-profile launch, the magazine did not do well. Quite by accident, Branson stumbled into the record business. Accounts of the launch of Virgin Records differ (Branson and his partner at first planned to call the company Slipped Disc Records, but they liked Virgin better because it connoted the naïveté of the owners and was slightly outrageous, a natural fit with the sixties), but as a result of one very successful advertisement, *Student* was soon in the mail-order record business.

Cash flow from the record business kept the magazine afloat until Branson lost interest in it and ceased its publication in order to focus on the record business. When a postal strike intervened to cut the young company's cash lifeline, Virgin responded by opening a record store. Crowds poured in, but costs were high and profit margins slim. Once again the company faced a cash crunch.

The Great Customs Scam

Branson found the answer to his latest dilemma again quite by accident. As he was attempting to transport a vanload of records to Belgium, French authorities at Calais sent him back across the English Channel because he didn't have the proper customs paperwork. As he groused about the French bureaucracy, he suddenly realized that he had a load of untaxed records, properly stamped at Dover for export, and the opportunity to sell them in London at regular prices. He could make close to $12,000 in extra profits by doing so.

His success with that venture led to what is known in Branson lore as "The Great Customs Scam." The first serendipitous phony export scheme lead to four additional trips in quick succession. According to an account of the event in the British edition of *GQ*, "Generally, Branson would fill the van with 'deletions'—old records by forgotten artists which could be bought cheaply—while at the same time ordering a consignment of new records ostensibly for export. The new records then went on to the shelves at Virgin's stores; the deletions were dumped at a municipal tip (dump) near Antwerp. The export stamp for the deletions provided a semblance of legality, or so it was thought.

"It was, in the end, an extraordinarily naive swindle. Nik Powell (Branson's boyhood friend and partner) was in the new Liverpool store, readying it for the grand opening, when Customs and Excise came to call. "They had an instrument, like a Geiger counter,' he recalls. 'Records for export had a sort of tag on them which this thing could read. They pointed at the stock and the machine went beserk. The customs guys were laughing out loud. We had to close the shop before it opened.' "[2]

A Salutary Experience

Branson was arrested and driven to Dover, where he was incarcerated until the next day, when his family could raise the $60,000 bail money by putting up their home as collateral. He felt horrible about the experience, he said, feeling as if he had really let his parents down. The case was dropped days before it went to court with Branson agreeing to pay about $30,000 in back taxes immediately with another $75,000 or so to be paid over the next three years. Branson summed up the experience for *GQ*. "It was, he said, a salutary experience. "I've never done anything in my life since then that I've felt I'd lose a night's sleep over,' he says simply."

The record stores prospered and evolved into a recording

---

studio and the Virgin record label. Branson's break into the big time came in 1973 as a result of his friendship with Mike Oldfield, who was a struggling composer at the time. Virgin recorded Mike Oldfield's ''Tubular Bells'' album, which eventually sold more than five million copies and established Virgin as a legitimate recording company. Phil Collins and Boy George signed on with Virgin. They were followed by other notables in the music business. Virgin Records has since grown into one of the top six record companies in the world and numbers among its artists: Paula Abdul, Bryan Ferry, Genesis, Phil Collins, Peter Gabriel, Steve Winwood, Joe Jackson, Lenny Kravitz, and most recently, Janet Jackson, and the Rolling Stones.

It is a source of pride to Branson that Virgin Records has never lost a major recording star, and most of them have become personal friends as well as business associates. In an interview in New York, he talked about skiing with Peter Gabriel, his long friendship with Phil Collins, and inadvertently dumping Janet Jackson in the woods in a hot air balloon. He also recalled the practical joke he played on Frank Zappa when he was driving Zappa to Virgin's recording studios in London. Branson dropped Zappa in front of a British mansion suggesting they meet inside after he parked the car. Zappa, assuming he was at Virgin's studios, rang the doorbell. He soon discovered that he had been left at Blenheim Palace, the home of the Duke of Marlborough.

Pranks aside, Virgin Records generated the cash that enabled Branson to start Virgin Atlantic, causing the British press to label it ''the airways that Boy George built.'' Branson's hijinks often mask his serious business side. He believes business should be fun, but it must be about building a worthwhile enterprise, creating jobs, and making money.

Minimizing Risk

''I don't like taking risks,'' he says. ''That sounds contradictory to the balloon thing, but I think that I'm protected against most of the downsides before going into something. With the airline, when we started it, we knew it was a very perilous business. We started with one plane in 1984 and we did a deal with Boeing that we could hand the plane back to them at the end of our first year if things didn't work out. That enabled us to put our toe in the water without putting everything at peril if we made a mistake.

"I think one has to accept that everything is probably not going to be great. An entrepreneur will take calculated risks and not everything he does will be successful. He is going to have to push himself and his people and his company forward. You put a toe in the water to see how it feels before you jump in," he says.

Daredevil Adventures

The "balloon thing" to which Branson referred is his penchant for daredevil adventures that have made him an international celebrity and his airline one of the most talked about in the industry, despite its relatively small size ($250 million in sales). His official biography provided by his company says: "Since 1985, Branson has been involved in a number of transoceanic, record-breaking attempts. In 1985, he attempted the first record-breaking crossing of the Atlantic Ocean since 1952 by speedboat. However, his Virgin Atlantic Challenger I sank a few miles from the completing of the crossing. In 1986 his boat, Virgin Atlantic Challenger II succeeded in crossing the Atlantic in the fastest recorded time ever.

"A year later, Richard Branson and his co-pilot, Per Lindstrand, successfully crossed the Atlantic for the first time in the history of hot air ballooning, in the largest hot air balloon ever built—the Virgin Atlantic Flyer. In 1990, Vice President Dan Quayle presented the two adventurers with the Harmon Aviation award in recognition of this achievement."

Definitely not describing your average CEO, Branson's corporate bio goes on, "In January 1991, Branson and Lindstrand successfully achieved the first crossing of the Pacific Ocean by hot air balloon in the Virgin Otsuka Pacific Flyer. Almost double the distance and doubly as treacherous as the Atlantic crossing, the pair broke their own existing ballooning records for speed, altitude, and distance."

There's more to the story. Branson's wife, Joan, had just given birth to their son, Sam, when his first transatlantic speedboat crashed into some debris and sank just 250 miles short of his goal and left Branson and the crew floating in the Atlantic. He made it on the second attempt.

Riding the Balloon Down

Perhaps that dunking influenced his decision to stay with the Virgin Atlantic Flyer when, after they had successfully crossed the Atlantic in a hot air balloon, Branson and copilot Lindstrand traveled 3,075 miles from Maine to the Irish Sea, farther than they had originally planned. They were scheduled to land in Ireland, but an untimely updraft propelled them upward and caused them to overshoot their mark.

"Per jumped into the sea and I was left with the out-of-control balloon," Branson recalled. "I had only actually learned to fly the plane two months before, so I wasn't really feeling too much in control. Standing on the top of the capsule, I wasn't even sure I had put my parachute on the right way and looking down at the clouds below . . . I had only done two parachute jumps in my life neither of which had been particularly successful. It was very lonely; the fuel was almost gone, and I was desperately trying to decide: Should I jump or shouldn't I?

An Important Decision

"In probably the most important decision of my life, I finally decided that if I was only going to live for a few more minutes, I would wait until the very last drop of fuel had been used up. I climbed back into the capsule to clear my mind and give myself time to think. I tried to decide if there was any alternative besides attempting to parachute into the sea at eight o'clock at night, which at the time didn't seem like a particularly good idea to me.

"My conclusion was that I would use the balloon as a parachute and not the parachute itself. I would ride the balloon down. When I came down through the clouds, somebody was very kind to me. I ran straight into a military exercise with helicopters everywhere. I jumped just before the balloon hit the water, and within minutes was picked up by a helicopter."

Less than four years later, Branson and Lindstrand were in an eight-foot pressurized capsule attached to an even larger balloon, the 220-foot-tall Pacific Flyer. Their plan was to fly from Miyakonojo on Japan's southern tip to California in a giant balloon tough enough to ride the jet stream, allowing them to break all ballooning speed records for a Pacific crossing.

Their spirits were high, and their confidence was bolstered by the earlier successful Atlantic crossing. The timing was not great; the United Nations deadline for Saddam Hussein to get his troops out of Kuwait was rapidly approaching and just two days earlier a Japanese balloonist had crashed four hundred miles short of his goal and died of exposure while awaiting rescue. But the jet stream was the best it had been all winter. Branson and Lindstrand decided to go.

Disaster over the Pacific

A thousand miles into the trip, they fired the explosive bolts designed to jettison the first used propane fuel tank. Suddenly, the capsule lurched wildly. The explosion had jettisoned all three tanks on one side of the balloon and the resulting tilt and upward acceleration resulting from the sudden loss of ballast left the remaining three tanks dangling precariously on the other side.

With half their fuel gone, options were limited. Ditching at sea while they were still in contact with Honolulu rescue seemed desirable. Problem was, surface winds were at gale force; ships in the area were having trouble holding their own in the rough seas. Their rescue coordinator told them they were very likely dead people if they ditched.

A Five Percent Chance

"We did our calculations and figured that the only way we could make it was to average 180 miles an hour," Branson recalled. He and Lindstrand figured they had maybe a five percent chance. The jet stream was their only hope. "We had done ninety miles an hour when we crossed the Atlantic so we knew that in order to average 180 we would have to get up to a speed of 300 miles an hour. So we went right to the core of the jet stream and the balloon just literally took off. Once again, somebody was kind to us. We managed to keep our averages up."

Flying at that speed, however, meant manually operating the

burner every minute of the trip. Lindstrand later told a Los Angeles *Times* reporter: "It's like driving a car on an icy road too fast for twenty-four hours." It was exhausting work. On the second night of the trip, as Branson slept, Lindstrand worked the controls. He looked up through the plastic bubble at the burners and thought he saw someone outside of the window looking in.

"Later, their roles were reversed when Branson noticed balls of flame above him. He kicked Lindstrand awake. 'Don't be stupid,' Lindstrand said. 'Nothing will burn up here.' It was fifty degrees below zero outside. Propane, which liquefies at minus-47, had formed little snowballs that ignited from the burner and were dropping onto the plastic canopy. 'Since we were pressurized, if that had ruptured the plastic, we would have just popped straight out in a very nasty ascent,' Branson said." They corrected the problem by switching burners.[3]

During the day, they used virtually no fuel. The balloon Lindstrand had designed and built worked better than they had hoped. They "solar-flew," as the heat from the sun heated the metallic surface of the balloon sufficiently to provide lift without using the burners. At times, they even had to open the parachute valve at the top of the balloon to keep it from rising.

Trouble persisted. Branson recalled: "A thousand miles from Los Angeles, the message came over: 'Some bad news for you. The winds have shifted and they are going to take you back to Japan, and you are flying over a force nine gale. The only possible chance you have is if you drop down to about ten thousand feet. There might be a wind that will blow you toward Canada.' "

A Wonderful Feeling

"It was quite remarkable," Branson said. "We dropped down to ten thousand feet and suddenly the balloon changed course, something that is very rare. You usually cannot choose your own destiny. You generally go wherever the wind blows

---

[3]Rich Roberts, "Floating Into a Nightmare," *Los Angeles Times*, 23 January 1991, Outdoors section.

you. We ended up landing two and one-half thousand miles from where we were planning to land, in a snowstorm, on a very, very remote frozen lake many miles from anywhere. It was a wonderful feeling!''

Where they were exactly was on an unnamed lake deep in Canada's frozen Northwest Territories. They had completed the longest manned balloon flight ever, flying sixty-seven hundred miles in forty-six hours and sixteen minutes at an average speed of 145 miles per hour.

Recalling his feelings later, Branson said, ''It wasn't fear of dying so much as it was a terrible feeling of loneliness. We had forty-six hours of thinking that we weren't going to survive, and that gives you plenty of time to think about life. I have always felt that one should live life to its fullest. Everybody does it in a sense, of course, but it depends on how you approach it. I love a challenge and I love to test myself and push myself as far as I can go. There's an element of youthful exuberance, as well, but I think that when it comes to doing something that man has not done before, you feel that somehow unless people are willing to push themselves, nothing goes forward.

Doing the Impossible

''There is obviously a risk that you may not come home from the adventure, but if you do, the satisfaction of having achieved it is very great. If we worry too much about the risk and not enough about the possibilities, a lot of things would never have happened. People said that it was impossible to fly a balloon in the jet stream, but we proved that it can be done.

''For me the adventure wasn't just the crossing, it was the preparation: getting to know the Japanese, spending six weeks in Miyakonojo, the training, getting close to the person I was going to do the adventure with, and the doing of something that was completely different from day-to-day problems. Suddenly those things don't seem quite so important. It's a wonderful break from everything else.''

Branson plans to stay home when the next great adventure is launched, although he is already in the planning stages of a transglobal hot air balloon flight that his company will sponsor. ''For the sake of my family and friends—and perhaps my sanity—I think I'll be staying on the ground. Perhaps I may finally have grown up.

A Paternal Lecture

''There is an element of selfishness in it. My wife and my parents have supported it generally, but after the Pacific crossing my father arranged a dinner to celebrate our success. He put me at the corner of the table so I couldn't escape and the whole family sat around the table and gave me my first lecture. My father said he had saved it until I was forty-one. It was quite powerful. He wouldn't let me out until I agreed not to go on the transglobal flight.''

Whether Branson is capable of keeping that promise as the lift-off date approaches remains to be seen, but he seems confident that Virgin Airways will provide quite enough challenges for the next few years. He's embroiled in a libel suit against arch-rival British Airways, charging the British giant with a variety of unfair competitive practices. He plans to see the suit through to the bitter end. (On January 11, 1993, British Airways admitted in court to conducting a dirty tricks campaign against Virgin, apologized to Branson and agreed to pay $2.5 million in damages and legal fees to end the libel suit.)[4]

In 1992, Branson sold Virgin Music Group to Thorn EMI, a British record label, for $980 million, an industry record. It was the last major deal in the industry because Virgin Records was at the time the largest independent label in the world. The conditions of the deal ensured that Virgin will remain independent within Thorn EMI, and that Branson will continue with the company as ''president for life.''

The cash generated by the sale of the record company will be invested in Virgin Airways. The company plans several major expansions during the 1990s, introducing service to new destinations in the U.S. and Africa and expanding service already provided to several cities. On the drawing boards are new routes to Singapore and Australia as well as expansion of Branson's hotel and other travel-related businesses.

---

[4]Paula Dwyer, ''British Air: Not Cricket,'' *Business Week* (January 25, 1993), 50–51.

Doing What He Likes

One gets the feeling that Branson is doing exactly what he would like to do with his life. When asked if he would continue to do what he does regardless of the money involved, he responded, "I think that most successful business people would say that they would do what they are doing whether there was any money in it or not. I am very fortunate to have a wonderfully rewarding and fascinating life and the variety is what makes it interesting.

"This week I've been to Barcelona to launch a new Virgin megastore that sells books and records, I've water skied behind our blimp, our new airship company that we started to promote our megastores, and I attended a charity function. The charity event was in a beautiful pitched tent that was wonderfully set up, and suddenly I had an idea to build a tented village as the head office for our airlines. We could get proper heating and air-conditioning for it and build it on a site we acquired before real estate values crashed. We could set up a lovely tented village—anyway, we've got two people looking into it.

Small Is Beautiful

"I think that if there is nothing else in my life, trying to run a small airline is enough of a challenge to keep me going for the next forty years. There are no small airlines that have ever survived. The big ones make sure of that. I suppose that is the principal challenge, but forty years from now I would like to have created the best companies in their world—not the biggest, the best. I think that you can't be the best if you're the biggest. If you talk to people who work for a small company, they are generally happy. With a large company, more often than not, I'm afraid, they are unhappy. There's always a danger that with a big company you simply become a number. I think in an ideal world all big companies would be split into ten or fourteen little companies. They shouldn't be allowed to go beyond a certain size. I think small is beautiful.

"At Virgin, we have the philosophy of not buying companies. I think one of the reasons we survived the eighties entrepreneurs crashing is that all our companies were started from scratch. It comes back down to people. If you buy a company, you would almost certainly have to lay off lots of people and you are buying someone else's philosophy. You get too big too quickly, whereas if you grow a company, you grow it in the way you want to see it grow. You make sure that the quality is of your particular standards and the people are the kind of people you want to have around you, and you know what you've got.

"Quite often, people have bought companies during the past ten years and they have made some horrendous mistakes, but the justification for buying companies is all too often to buy them, merge them, lay people off and make it a profitable business. That might make sense from a balance sheet point of view, but it is a very cold-hearted way of living. There is a great deal more satisfaction in building something from scratch and seeing it work. It's like having a baby and the satisfaction that comes from being a parent.

Living a Happy Life

"Last night over drinks with the crew we were talking about what's important in life. I think most companies and most people forget that having a good time is very important. When companies forget it, people won't enjoy life. I think having a happy life is more important than having a few good friends. I would like to live so that when I reach the age of eighty or ninety, I can look back and feel quite pleased and happy with the life I've lived.

"I think being happy means going into a profession not for the money, but for the personal satisfaction one gets from it. This may mean indulging your hobby to make it into a business. My daughter takes a lot of photographs and I think the idea of her one day becoming a photographer would be wonderful, meeting lots of people and traveling, if that's what she wants to do. That is the best possible combination—when your hobby and your work are the same thing.

"Balance is obviously very important. I think being fit and healthy is important, because if your body is fit and healthy, you are going to be able to make more rational decisions. Therefore, you've got to find the time to stay fit, to play as well as to work, and to recharge your batteries. I'm particularly lucky in that my work is like play to me anyway, and the need to do something different is not as great as it might be for some people. I only go into businesses for the pleasure of doing it, not for the money. It's the pleasure of creating something better than anyone else has ever done as well as the pleasure of dealing with the people in the business.

"I have time to spend with my children. Kids need their parents, and it's very important to spend time with them. A family is also good to help keep one's feet on the ground. I am quite lucky that my wife is very much a working-class lady who lived with six people in a bed until she was fifteen or sixteen and very, very down-to-earth. If my head gets a bit big, she very soon puts me in my place. If I come home with something great that I have done that day, she'll be completely and utterly unimpressed. She'll say, "Right. Why don't you change the baby's nappies (diapers) or something.' We have a good partnership. She keeps me in balance."

Striving for Balance

Laughs Lori Levin-Hyams, Virgin's U.S. director of public relations, "Richard is in balance because he's mastered the art of delegation. The rest of us are loaded up and out of balance, but Richard's fine! I hope you include something in your book about women and how difficult it is to juggle a family, a career, and everything else."

I hope the book does, indeed, offer hope to all of us who are trying to find the right balance for our lives. It started out as a book about the importance of achieving balance in one's life, but somewhere along the way, it became a book about the importance of *striving* for balance. Perfect balance may never be achieved. The important thing is the trying. It's not the destination that makes the journey meaningful, it's the experiences along the way that make the trip worthwhile.

Key Points and Action Items

1. Most of us have done things we regret later. Make it a practice to learn from your mistakes, correct them, and never again do anything that would cause you to lose a night's sleep.

2. Don't avoid risk. Minimize it. Protect yourself against the downside while positioning yourself to take advantage of the upside. Explore options that allow you to put a toe in the water without placing everything at peril.

3. There are few crises that require instantaneous action. When you are faced with a difficult decision, take time to clear your mind and give yourself time to think through the options.

4. If we worry too much about the risk and not enough about the possibilities, a lot of things will never happen. The trick is to find the right balance.

5. There are always those who are quick to point out that something cannot be done. But, when it comes to doing something that no one has ever done before, unless we are willing to push ourselves, nothing goes forward.